UNIVERSE

Britannica Illustrated Science Library

Encyclopædia Britannica, Inc.
Chicago ▪ London ▪ New Delhi ▪ Paris ▪ Seoul ▪ Sydney ▪ Taipei ▪ Tokyo

Britannica Illustrated Science Library

© 2008 Editorial Sol 90

Idea and Concept of This Work: Editorial Sol 90

Project Management: Fabián Cassan

Photo Credits: Corbis, ESA, Getty Images, Graphic News, NASA, National Geographic, Science Photo Library

Illustrators: Guido Arroyo, Pablo Aschei, Gustavo J. Caironi, Hernán Cañellas, Leonardo César, José Luis Corsetti, Vanina Farías, Joana Garrido, Celina Hilbert, Isidro López, Diego Martín, Jorge Martínez, Marco Menco, Ala de Mosca, Diego Mourelos, Eduardo Pérez, Javier Pérez, Ariel Piroyansky, Ariel Roldán, Marcel Socías, Néstor Taylor, Trebol Animation, Juan Venegas, Coralia Vignau, 3DN, 3DOM studio

Composition and Pre-press Services: Editorial Sol 90

Translation Services and Index: Publication Services, Inc.

Britannica Illustrated Science Library Staff

Editorial
Michael Levy, *Executive Editor, Core Editorial*
John Rafferty, *Associate Editor, Earth Sciences*
William L. Hosch, *Associate Editor, Mathematics and Computers*
Kara Rogers, *Associate Editor, Life Sciences*
Rob Curley, *Senior Editor, Science and Technology*
David Hayes, *Special Projects Editor*

Art and Composition
Steven N. Kapusta, *Director*
Carol A. Gaines, *Composition Supervisor*
Christine McCabe, *Senior Illustrator*

Media Acquisition
Kathy Nakamura, *Manager*

Copy Department
Sylvia Wallace, *Director*
Julian Ronning, *Supervisor*

Information Management and Retrieval
Sheila Vasich, *Information Architect*

Production Control
Marilyn L. Barton

Manufacturing
Kim Gerber, *Director*

Encyclopædia Britannica, Inc.

Jacob E. Safra, *Chairman of the Board*

Jorge Aguilar-Cauz, *President*

Michael Ross, *Senior Vice President, Corporate Development*

Dale H. Hoiberg, *Senior Vice President and Editor*

Marsha Mackenzie, *Director of Production*

International Standard Book Number (set):
  978-1-59339-382-3
International Standard Book Number (volume):
  978-1-59339-399-1
Britannica Illustrated Science Library: Universe 2008

Printed in China

www.britannica.com

Universe

Contents

The Secrets of the Universe

There was a time when people believed that the stars were bonfires lit by other tribes in the sky, that the universe was a flat plate resting on the shell of a giant turtle, and that the Earth, according to the Greek astronomer Ptolemy, was at the center of the universe. From the most remote of times, people have been curious about what lies hidden beyond the celestial sphere. This curiosity has led them to build telescopes that show with clarity otherwise blurry and distant objects. In this book you will find the history of the cosmos illustrated with spectacular images that show in detail how the cosmos was formed, the nature of the many points of light that adorn the night sky, and what lies ahead. You will also discover how the suns that inhabit space live and die, what dark matter and black holes are, and what our place is in this vastness. Certainly, the opportunity to compare the destiny of other worlds similar to ours will help us understand that for the time being there is no better place than the Earth to live. At least for now.

n the Milky Way—according to mathematical and physical calculations—there are more than 100 billion stars, and such a multitude leads to the question: Is it possible that our Sun is the only star that possesses an inhabited planet? Astronomers are more convinced than ever of the possibility of life in other worlds. We just need to find them. Reading this book will let you become better acquainted with our neighbors in the solar system—the other planets—and the most important characteristics that distinguish them. All this information that explores the mysteries of space is accompanied by recent images captured by the newest telescopes. They reveal many details about the planets and their satellites, such as the volcanoes and craters found on the surface of some of them. You will also learn more about the asteroids and comets that orbit the Sun and about Pluto, a dwarf planet, which is to be visited by a space probe for the first time. Less than a decade ago, astronomers began observing frozen worlds, much smaller than a planet, in a region of the solar system called the Kuiper belt. We invite you to explore all of this. The images and illustrations that accompany the text will prove very helpful in studying and understanding the structure of all the visible and invisible objects (such as dark matter) that form part of the universe. There are stellar maps showing the constellations, the groups of stars that since ancient times have served as a guide for navigation and for the development of calendars. There is also a review through history: from Ptolemy, who thought the planets orbited around the Earth, and Copernicus, who put the Sun in the center, and Galileo, the first to aim a telescope skyward, up to the most recent astronomical theories, such as those of Stephen Hawking, the genius of space and time who continues to amaze with his discoveries about the greatest mysteries of the cosmos. You will find these and many more topics no matter where you look in this fantastic book that puts the universe and its secrets in your hands.

What Is the Universe?

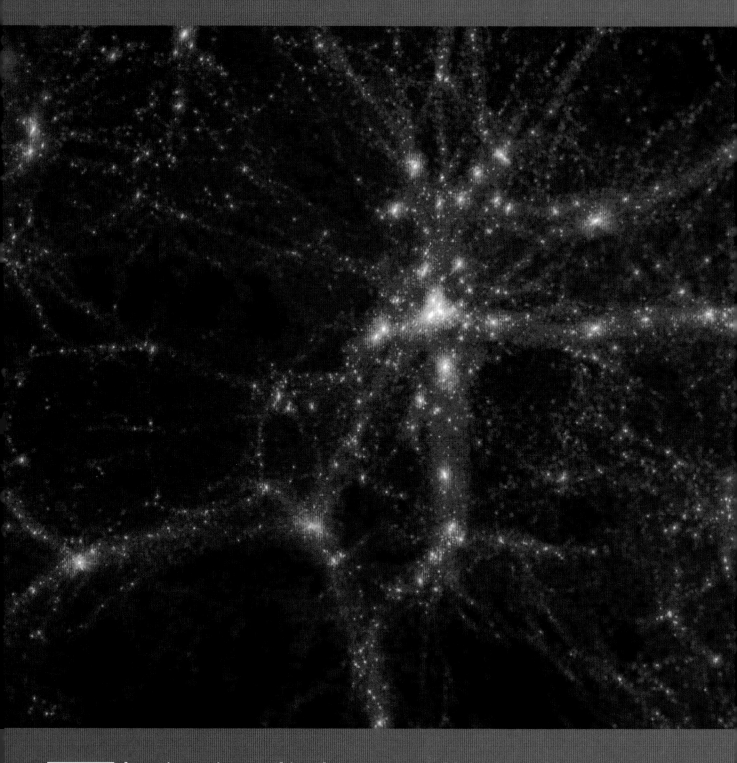

The universe is everything that exists, from the smallest particles to the largest ones, together with all matter and energy. The universe includes visible and invisible things, such as dark matter, the great, secret component of the cosmos. The search for dark matter is currently one of the most important tasks of cosmology. Dark matter may

DARK MATTER
Evidence exists that dark matter, though invisible
to telescopes, betrays itself by the gravitational
pull it exerts over other heavenly bodies.

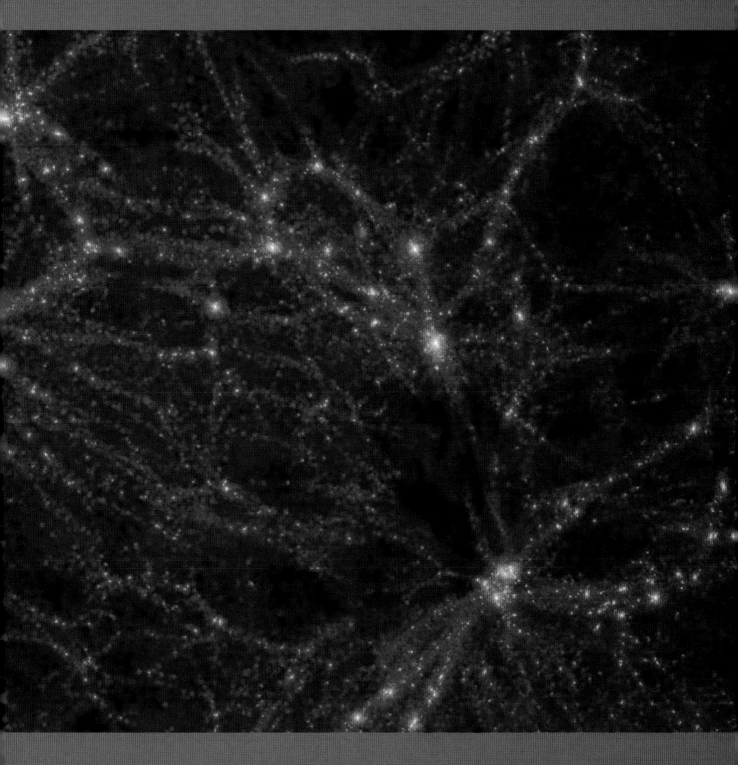

literally determine the density of all of space, as well as decide the destiny of the universe. Did you know that, second by second, the universe grows and grows? The question that astronomers are asking—the question that concerns them the most—is how much longer the universe can continue to expand like a balloon before turning into something cold and dark. ●

X-Ray of the Cosmos

T he universe, marvelous in its majesty, is an ensemble of a hundred billion galaxies. Each of these galaxies (which tend to be found in large groups) has billions of stars. These galactic concentrations surround empty spaces, called cosmic voids. The immensity of the cosmos can be better grasped by realizing that the size of our fragile planet Earth, or even that of the Milky Way, is insignificant compared to the size of the remainder of the cosmos. ◉

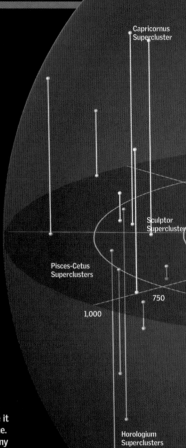

Capricornus Supercluster

Sculptor Supercluster

Pisces-Cetus Superclusters

750

1,000

Horologium Superclusters

1.

EARTH Originated, together with the solar system, when the universe was already 9.1 billion years old. It is the only known planet that is home to life.

EARTH
Neptune
Uranus
Pluto
Jupiter
Saturn

The Universe

▶ Originating nearly 14 billion years ago in an immense explosion, the universe today is too large to be able to conceive. The innumerable stars and galaxies that populate it promise to continue expanding for a long time. Though it might sound strange today, for many years, astronomers thought that the Milky Way, where the Earth is located, constituted the entire universe. Only recently—in the 20th century—was outer space recognized as not only much vaster than previously thought but also as being in a state of ongoing expansion.

2.

NEAR STARS Found closer than 20 light-years from the Sun, they make up our solar neighborhood.

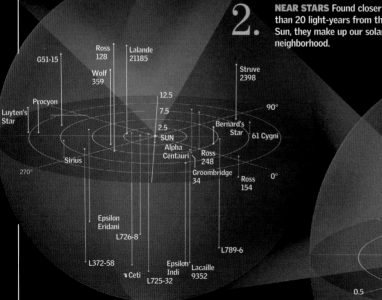

G51-15
Ross 128
Lalande 21185
Wolf 359
Struve 2398
Procyon
12.5
7.5
90°
Luyten's Star
2.5
Bernard's Star
61 Cygni
SUN
Alpha Centauri
Ross 248
Sirius
Groombridge 34
Ross 154
0°
270°
Epsilon Eridani
L726-8
L789-6
L372-58
Epsilon Indi
Lacaille 9352
τ Ceti
L725-32

3.

NEIGHBORS Within a space of one million light-years, we find the Milky Way and its closest galaxies.

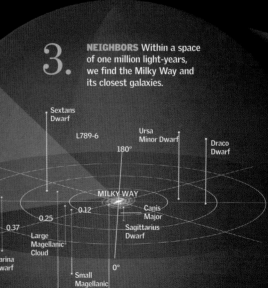

Sextans Dwarf
L789-6
Ursa Minor Dwarf
180°
Draco Dwarf
MILKY WAY
0.12
0.25
Canis Major
Sagittarius Dwarf
0.37
0.5
Large Magellanic Cloud
Carina Dwarf
0°
Small Magellanic Cloud

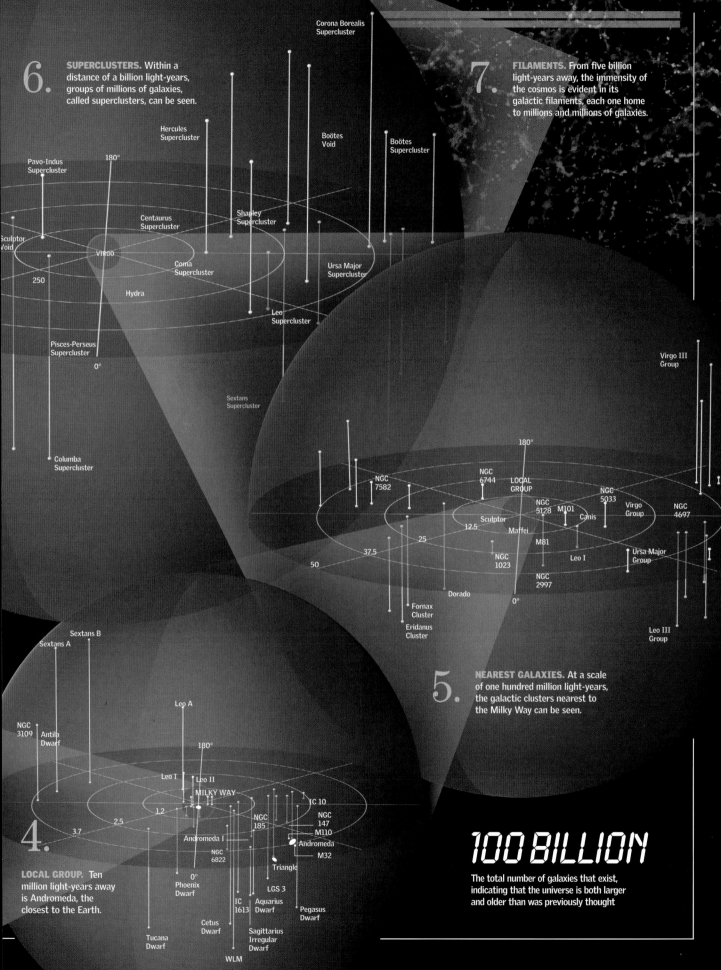

6. **SUPERCLUSTERS.** Within a distance of a billion light-years, groups of millions of galaxies, called superclusters, can be seen.

Corona Borealis Supercluster

Hercules Supercluster

Boötes Void

Boötes Supercluster

Pavo-Indus Supercluster

180°

Sculptor Void

Centaurus Supercluster

Shapley Supercluster

VIRGO

Coma Supercluster

250

Hydra

Ursa Major Supercluster

Leo Supercluster

Pisces-Perseus Supercluster

0°

Sextans Supercluster

Columba Supercluster

7. **FILAMENTS.** From five billion light-years away, the immensity of the cosmos is evident in its galactic filaments, each one home to millions and millions of galaxies.

Virgo III Group

180°

NGC 6744

LOCAL GROUP

NGC 5033

NGC 7582

NGC 5128

M101

Virgo Group

NGC 4697

Sculptor

Canis

12.5

Maffei

M81

25

Ursa Major Group

37.5

NGC 1023

Leo I

50

NGC 2997

Dorado

NGC 2997

0°

Fornax Cluster

Eridanus Cluster

Leo III Group

5. **NEAREST GALAXIES.** At a scale of one hundred million light-years, the galactic clusters nearest to the Milky Way can be seen.

Sextans B

Sextans A

Leo A

NGC 3109

Antila Dwarf

180°

Leo I

Leo II

MILKY WAY

IC 10

1.2

NGC 185

NGC 147

M110

2.5

Andromeda I

Andromeda

3.7

NGC 6822

M32

Triangle

4.

0°

Phoenix Dwarf

LGS 3

Pegasus Dwarf

LOCAL GROUP. Ten million light-years away is Andromeda, the closest to the Earth.

IC 1613

Aquarius Dwarf

Tucana Dwarf

Cetus Dwarf

Sagittarius Irregular Dwarf

WLM

100 BILLION

The total number of galaxies that exist, indicating that the universe is both larger and older than was previously thought

The Instant of Creation

t is impossible to know precisely how, out of nothing, the universe began to exist. According to the big bang theory—the theory most widely accepted in the scientific community—in the beginning, there appeared an infinitely small and dense burning ball that gave rise to space, matter, and energy. This happened 13.7 billion years ago. The great, unanswered question is what caused a small dot of light—filled with concentrated energy from which matter and antimatter were created—to arise from nothingness. In very little time, the young universe began to expand and cool. Several billion years later, it acquired the form we know today.

HOW IT GREW

Cosmic inflation was an expansion of the entire universe. The Earth's galactic neighborhood appears fairly uniform. Everywhere you look, the types of galaxies and the background temperature are essentially the same.

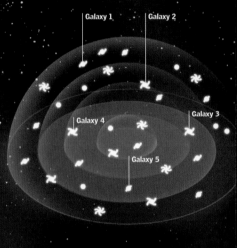

Galaxy 1 Galaxy 2
Galaxy 3
Galaxy 4
Galaxy 5

Energetic Radiation

The burning ball that gave rise to the universe remained a source of permanent radiation. Subatomic particles and antiparticles annihilated each other. The ball's high density spontaneously produced matter and destroyed it. Had this state of affairs continued, the universe would never have undergone the growth that scientists believe followed cosmic inflation.

TIME	**0**	10^{-43} sec	10^{-38} sec
TEMPERATURE	–	10^{32} ° F (and C)	10^{29} ° F (and C)

1 Scientists theorize that, from nothing, something infinitely small, dense, and hot appeared. All that exists today was compressed into a ball smaller than the nucleus of an atom.

2 At the closest moment to zero time, which physics has been able to reach, the temperature is extremely high. Before the universe's inflation, a superforce governed everything.

3 The universe is unstable. Only 10^{-38} seconds after the big bang, the universe increases in size more than a trillion trillion times. The expansion of the universe and the division of its forces be

ELEMENTARY PARTICLES

In its beginnings, the universe was a soup of particles that interacted with each other because of high levels of radiation. Later, as the universe expanded, quarks formed the nuclei of the elements and then joined with electrons to form atoms.

Photon
Massless elemental luminous particle

Gluon
Responsible for the interactions between quarks

Electron
Negatively charged elemental particle

Graviton
It is believed to transmit gravitation.

Quark
Light, elemental particle

Cosmic Inflation Theory

▶ Although big bang theorists understood the universe as originating in an extremely small, hot, and condensed ball, they could not understand the reason for its staggering growth. In 1981, physicist Alan Guth proposed a solution to the problem with his inflationary theory. In an extremely short period of time (less than a thousandth of a second), the universe grew more than a trillion trillion trillion times. Near the end of this period of expansion, the temperature approached absolute zero.

WMAP (WILKINSON MICROWAVE ANISOTROPY PROBE)

NASA's WMAP project maps the background radiation of the universe. In the image, hotter (red-yellow) regions and colder (blue-green) regions can be observed. WMAP makes it possible to determine the amount of dark matter.

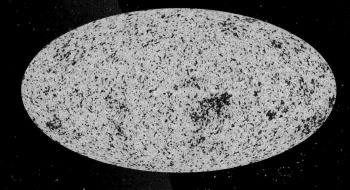

HOW IT DID NOT GROW

Had the universe not undergone inflation, it would be a collection of different regions, each with its own particular types of galaxies and each nearly distinguishable from the others.

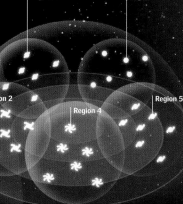

Region 1
Region 3
Region 2
Region 4
Region 5

THE SEPARATION OF FORCES

Before the universe expanded, during a period of radiation, only one unified force governed all physical interactions. The first distinguishable force was gravity, followed by electromagnetism and nuclear interactions. Upon the division of the universe's forces, matter was created.

Gravity
Strong nuclear
Weak nuclear
Electromagnetism
SUPERFORCE
EXPANSION

10^{-12} sec

$10^{15}\,°\ F\ (and\ C)$

4 The universe experiences a gigantic cooldown. Gravity has already become distinguishable, and the electromagnetic force and the strong and weak nuclear interactions appear.

10^{-4} sec

$10^{12}\,°\ F\ (and\ C)$

5 Protons and neutrons appear, formed by three quarks apiece. Because all light is trapped within the web of particles, the universe is still dark.

5 sec

$9 \times 10^{9}\,°\ F\ (5 \times 10^{9}\,°\ C)$

6 The electrons and their antiparticles, positrons, annihilate each other until the positrons disappear. The remaining electrons form atoms.

3 min

$2 \times 10^{9}\,°\ F\ (1 \times 10^{9}\,°\ C)$

7 The nuclei of the lightest elements, hydrogen and helium, form. Protons and neutrons unite to form the nuclei of atoms.

1 sec

The neutrinos separate from the initial particle soup through the disintegration of neutrons. Though having extremely little mass, the neutrinos might nevertheless form the greatest part of the universe's dark matter.

FROM PARTICLES TO MATTER

The quarks, among the oldest particles, interact with each other by forces transmitted through gluons. Later protons and neutrons will join to form nuclei.

Quark
Gluon

1 A gluon interacts with a quark.

2 Quarks join by means of gluons to form protons and neutrons.

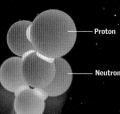

Proton
Neutron

3 Protons and neutrons unite to create nuclei.

The Transparent Universe

With the creation of atoms and overall cooling, the once opaque and dense universe became transparent. Electrons were attracted by the protons of hydrogen and helium nuclei, and together they formed atoms. Photons (massless particles of light) could now pass freely through the universe. With the cooling, radiation remained abundant but was no longer the sole governing factor of the universe. Matter, through gravitational force, could now direct its own destiny. The gaseous lumps that were present in this process grew larger and larger. After 100 million years, they formed even larger objects. Their shapes not yet defined, they constituted protogalaxies. Gravitation gave shape to the first galaxies some 500 million years after the big bang, and the first stars began to shine in the densest regions of these galaxies. One mystery that could not be solved was why galaxies were distributed and shaped the way they were. The solution that astronomers have been able to find through indirect evidence is that there exists material called dark matter whose presence would have played a role in galaxy formation.

1 Gaseous cloud
The first gases and dust resulting from the Big Bang form a cloud.

2 First filaments
Because of the gravitational pull of dark matter, the gases joined in the form of filaments.

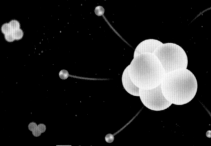

DARK MATTER

The visible objects in the cosmos represent only a small fraction of the total matter within the universe. Most of it is invisible even to the most powerful telescopes. Galaxies and their stars move as they do because of the gravitational forces exerted by this material, which astronomers call dark matter.

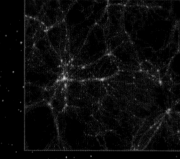

EVOLUTION OF MATTER

What can be observed in the universe today is a great quantity of matter grouped into galaxies. But that was not the original form of the universe. What the big bang initially produced was a cloud of uniformly dispersed gas. Just three million years later, the gas began to organize itself into filaments. Today the universe can be seen as a network of galactic filaments with enormous voids between them.

TIME (in years)	380,000	500 million
TEMPERATURE	4,900° F (2,700° C)	-405° F (-243° C)

8 380,000 years after the big bang, atoms form. Electrons orbit the nuclei, attracted by the protons. The universe becomes transparent. Photons travel through space.

9 Galaxies acquire their definitive shape: islands of millions and millions of stars and masses of gases and dust. The stars explode as supernovas and disperse heavier elements, such as carbon.

FIRST ATOMS

Hydrogen and helium were the first elements to be formed at the atomic level. They are the main components of stars and planets. They are by far the most abundant elements in the universe.

NUCLEUS 1 | Proton

Electron

Neutron

NUCLEUS 2

1 Hydrogen
An electron is attracted by and orbits the nucleus, which has a proton and a neutron.

2 Helium
Since the nucleus has two protons, two electrons are attracted to it.

3 Carbon
With time, heavier and more complex elements were formed. Carbon, the key to human life, has six protons in its nucleus and six electrons orbiting it.

3 Filament networks
The universe has
large-scale filaments
that contain millions
and millions of galaxies.

THE UNIVERSE TODAY

Star
cluster

Star

Nebula

Irregular
galaxy

Quasar

Spiral
galaxy

Barred
spiral
galaxy

Elliptical
galaxy

Galaxy
cluster

9.1 billion
THE EARTH IS CREATED
Like the rest of the planets, the Earth is made of
material that remained after the formation of the solar
system. The Earth is the only planet known to have life.

9 billion

-432° F (-258° C)

10 Nine billion years after the big
bang, the solar system
emerged. A mass of gas and
dust collapsed until it gave rise
to the Sun. Later the planetary system was
formed from the leftover material.

13.7 billion

-454° F (-270° C)

11 The universe continues to expand. Countless galaxies
are surrounded by dark matter, which represents 22
percent of the mass and energy in the universe. The
ordinary matter, of which stars and planets are
made, represents just 4 percent of the total. The predominant
form of energy is also of an unknown type. Called dark energy, it
constitutes 74 percent of the total mass and energy.

TIMESCALE
The vast span of time related to the history of
the universe can be readily understood if it is
scaled to correspond to a single year—a year
that spans the beginning of the universe, the

appearance of humans on the Earth, and the
voyage of Columbus to America. On January 1
of this imaginary year—at midnight—the big
bang takes place. *Homo sapiens* appears at

11:56 P.M. on December 31, and Columbus sets
sail on the last second of the last day of the
year. One second on this timescale is equivalent
to 500 true years.

BIG BANG
occurs on the
first second of
the first day of
the year.

THE SOLAR
SYSTEM
is created on
August 24 of
this timescale.

COLUMBUS'S
ARRIVAL
takes place on
the last second
of December 31.

JANUARY

DECEMBER

Everything Comes to an End

The big bang theory helped solve the enigma of the early moments of the universe. What has yet to be resolved is the mystery surrounding the future that awaits. To unravel this mystery, the total mass of the universe must be known, but that figure has not yet been reliably determined. The most recent observations have removed some of this uncertainty. It seems that the mass of the universe is far too little to stop its expansion. If this is this case, the universe's present growth is merely the last step before its total death in complete darkness.

Flat Universe

1 There is a critical amount of mass for which the universe would expand at a declining rate without ever totally stopping. The result of this eternal expansion would be the existence of an ever-increasing number of galaxies and stars. If the universe were flat, we could talk about a cosmos born from an explosion, but it would be a universe continuing outward forever. It is difficult to think about a universe with these characteristics.

1 The universe continuously expands and evolves.

2 The universe's expansion is unceasing but ever slower.

3 Gravity is not sufficient to bring a complete stop to the universe's expansion.

4 The universe expands indefinitely.

THE HAWKING UNIVERSE
The universe was composed originally of four spatial dimensions without the dimension of time. Since there is no change without time, one of these dimensions, according to Hawking, transformed spontaneously on a small scale into a temporal dimension, and the universe began to expand.

Object in three dimensions

Object that changes with time

BIG BANG

1 After the original expansion, the universe grows.

2 Expansion is continuous and pronounced.

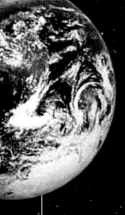

Closed Universe

2 If the universe had more than critical mass, it would expand until reaching a point where gravity stopped the expansion. Then, the universe would contract in the Big Crunch, a total collapse culminating in an infinitely small, dense, and hot spot similar to the one from which the universe was formed. Gravity's pull on the universe's excess matter would stop the expansion and reverse the process.

BIG CRUNCH

1 The universe expands violently.

2 The universe's growth slows.

3 The universe collapses upon itself, forming a dense, hot spot.

HOW IT IS MADE UP
Dark energy is hypothesized to be the predominant energy in the universe. It is believed to speed up the expansion of the universe.

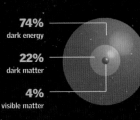

74%
dark energy

22%
dark matter

4%
visible matter

DISCOVERIES

The key discovery that led to the big bang theory was made in the early 1920s by Edwin Hubble, who discovered that galaxies were moving away from each other. In the 1940s, George Gamow developed the idea that the universe began with a primordial explosion. A consequence of such an event would be the existence of background radiation, which Arno Penzias and Robert Wilson accidentally detected in the mid-1960s.

1920s
GALACTIC EXPANSION
By noting a redshift toward the red end of the spectrum, Hubble was able to demonstrate that galaxies were moving away from each other.

1940s
GAMOW'S SUSPICION
Gamow first hypothesized the big bang, holding that the early universe was a "cauldron" of particles.

1965
BACKGROUND RADIATION
Penzias and Wilson detected radio signals that came from across the entire sky—the uniform signal of background radiation.

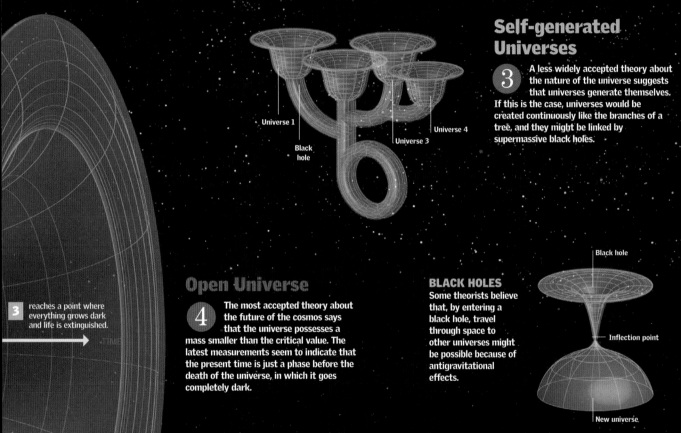

Self-generated Universes

3 A less widely accepted theory about the nature of the universe suggests that universes generate themselves. If this is the case, universes would be created continuously like the branches of a tree, and they might be linked by supermassive black holes.

Universe 1
Black hole
Universe 3
Universe 4

3 reaches a point where everything grows dark and life is extinguished.

TIME

Open Universe

4 The most accepted theory about the future of the cosmos says that the universe possesses a mass smaller than the critical value. The latest measurements seem to indicate that the present time is just a phase before the death of the universe, in which it goes completely dark.

BLACK HOLES

Some theorists believe that, by entering a black hole, travel through space to other universes might be possible because of antigravitational effects.

Black hole
Inflection point
New universe

Universe 1
Universe 2
Universe 3

Baby Universes

5 According to this theory, universes continuously sprout other universes. But in this case, one universe would be created from the death or disappearance of another. Each dead universe in a final collapse, or Big Crunch, would give rise to a supermassive black hole, from which another universe would be born. This process could repeat itself indefinitely, making the number of universes impossible to determine.

The Forces of the Universe

The four fundamental forces of nature are those that are not derived from basic forces. Physicists believe that, at one time, all physical forces functioned as a single force and that during the expansion of the universe, they became distinct from each other. Each force now governs different processes, and each interaction affects different types of particles. Gravity, electromagnetism, strong nuclear interactions, and weak nuclear interactions are essential to our understanding of the behavior of the many objects that exist in the universe. In recent years, many scientists have tried with little success to show how all forces are manifestations of a single type of exchange.

General Theory of Relativity

The biggest contribution to our comprehension of the universe's internal workings was made by Albert Einstein in 1915. Building on Newton's theory of universal gravitation, Einstein thought of space as linked to time. To Newton, gravity was merely the force that attracted two objects, but Einstein hypothesized that it was a consequence of what he called the curvature of space-time. According to his general theory of relativity, the universe curves in the presence of objects with mass. Gravity, according to this theory, is a distortion of space that determines whether one object rolls toward another. Einstein's general theory of relativity required scientists to consider the universe in terms of a non-Euclidian geometry, since it is not compatible with the idea of a flat universe. In Einsteinian space, two parallel lines can meet.

What we see

Real position

LUMINOUS TRAJECTORY

Positive pole

$$E=mc^2$$

In Einstein's equation, energy and mass are interchangeable. If an object increases its mass, its energy increases, and vice versa.

SUN

EARTH

Gravity

1 Gravity was the first force to become distinguishable from the original superforce. Today scientists understand gravity in Einstein's terms as an effect of the curvature of space-time. If the universe were thought of as a cube, the presence of any object with mass in space would deform the cube. Gravity can act at great distances (just as electromagnetism can) and always exerts a force of attraction. Despite the many attempts to find antigravity (which could counteract the effects of black holes), it has yet to be found.

Negative pole

The universe, if it were empty, could be pictured in this way.

The universe is deformed by the mass of the objects it contains.

UNIVERSAL GRAVITATION

The gravitation proposed by Newton is the mutual attraction between bodies having mass. The equation developed by Newton to calculate this force states that the attraction experienced by two bodies is directly proportional to the product of their masses and inversely proportional to the square of the distance between them. Newton represented the constant of proportionality resulting from this interaction as G. The shortcoming of Newton's law, an accepted paradigm until Einstein's theory of general relativity, lies in its failure to make time an essential component in the interaction between objects. According to Newton, the gravitational attraction between two objects with mass did not depend on the properties of space but was an intrinsic property of the objects themselves. Nevertheless, Newton's law of universal gravitation was a foundation for Einstein's theory.

NEWTON'S EQUATION

Two bodies with mass attract each other. Whichever body has the greatest mass will exert a greater force on the other. The greater the distance between the objects, the smaller the force they exert on each other.

$$F = \dfrac{G \times m1 \times m2}{d^2}$$

Strong Nuclear Force

3 The strong nuclear force holds the protons and neutrons of atomic nuclei together. Both protons and neutrons are subject to this force. Gluons are particles that carry the strong nuclear force, and they bind quarks together to form protons and neutrons. Atomic nuclei are held together by residual forces in the interaction between quarks and gluons.

1 Quarks and gluons
The strong nuclear interaction takes place when the gluon interacts with quarks.

Nucleus

Quark

Force
Gluon

2 Union
Quarks join and form nuclear protons and neutrons.

Electromagnetism

2 Electromagnetism is the force that affects electrically charged bodies. It is involved in the chemical and physical transformations of the atoms and molecules of the various elements. The electromagnetic force can be one of attraction or repulsion, with two types of charges or poles.

Attraction
Two atoms are drawn together, and the electrons rotate around the new molecule.

Hydrogen

Helium

Force

Electron

Positive pole

Nucleus

Negative pole

MOLECULAR MAGNETISM
In atoms and molecules, the electromagnetic force is dominant. It is the force that causes the attraction between protons and electrons in an atom and the attraction or repulsion between ionized atoms.

BENDING LIGHT
Light also bends because of the curvature of space-time. When seen from a telescope, the real position of an object is distorted. What is perceived through the telescope is a false location, generated by the curvature of the light. It is not possible to see the actual position of the object.

Weak Nuclear Force

4 The weak nuclear force is not as strong as the other forces. The weak nuclear interaction influences the beta decay of a neutron, which releases a proton and a neutrino that later transforms into an electron. This force takes part in the natural radioactive phenomena associated with certain types of atoms.

1 Hydrogen
A hydrogen atom interacts with a weak, light particle (WIMP). A neutron's bottom quark transforms into a top quark.

HELIUM ISOTOPE

Electron

Proton

HYDROGEN ATOM

Proton

Electron

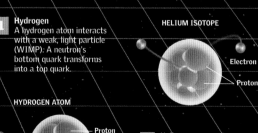

2 Helium
The neutron transforms into a proton. An electron is released, and the helium isotope that is formed has no nuclear neutrons.

Neutron

WIMP

What Is in the Universe?

The universe is populated on a grand scale by strands of superclusters surrounding vacant areas. Sometimes the galaxies collide with each other, triggering the formation of stars. In the vast cosmos, there are also quasars, pulsars, and black holes. Thanks to current technology, we can enjoy the displays of light and shadow

ETA CARINAE NEBULA
With a diameter of more than 200 light-years, it is one of biggest and brightest nebulae of our galaxy. This young, supermassive star is expected to become a supernova in the near future.

that make up, for example, the Eta Carinae Nebula (shown), which is composed of jets of hot, fluorescent gases. Although not all the objects in the universe are known, it can be said without a doubt that most of the atoms that make up our bodies have been born in the interior of stars. ●

Luminous

For a long time stars were a mystery to humans, and it was only as recently as the 19th century that astronomers began to understand the true nature of stars. Today we know that they are gigantic spheres of incandescent gas—mostly hydrogen, with a smaller proportion of helium. As a star radiates light, astronomers can precisely measure its brightness, color, and temperature. Because of their enormous distance from the Earth, stars beyond the Sun only appear as points of light, and even the most powerful telescopes do not reveal any surface features. ●

Hertzsprung-Russell (H-R) Diagram

The H-R diagram plots the intrinsic luminosity of stars against their spectral class, which corresponds to their temperature or the wavelengths of light they emit. The most massive stars are those with greatest intrinsic luminosity. They include blue stars, red giants, and red supergiants. Stars spend 90 percent of their lives in what is known as the main sequence.

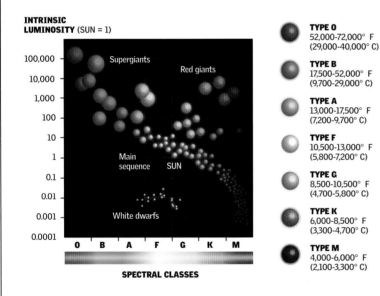

INTRINSIC LUMINOSITY (SUN = 1)

- Supergiants
- Red giants
- Main sequence
- SUN
- White dwarfs

100,000
10,000
1,000
100
10
1
0.1
0.01
0.001
0.0001

O B A F G K M

SPECTRAL CLASSES

TYPE O
52,000-72,000° F
(29,000-40,000° C)

TYPE B
17,500-52,000° F
(9,700-29,000° C)

TYPE A
13,000-17,500° F
(7,200-9,700° C)

TYPE F
10,500-13,000° F
(5,800-7,200° C)

TYPE G
8,500-10,500° F
(4,700-5,800° C)

TYPE K
6,000-8,500° F
(3,300-4,700° C)

TYPE M
4,000-6,000° F
(2,100-3,300° C)

Light-years and Parsecs

In measuring the great distances between stars, both light-years (ly) and parsecs (pc) are used. A light-year is the distance that light travels in a year— 5.9 trillion miles (10 trillion km). A light-year is a unit of distance, not time. A parsec is equivalent to the distance between the star and the Earth if the parallax angle is of one second arc. A pc is equal to 3.26 light-years, or 19 trillion miles (31 trillion km).

COLORS The hottest stars are bluish-white (spectral classes O, B, and A). The coolest stars are orange, yellow, and red (spectral classes G, K, and M).

PRINCIPAL STARS WITHIN 100 LY FROM THE SUN

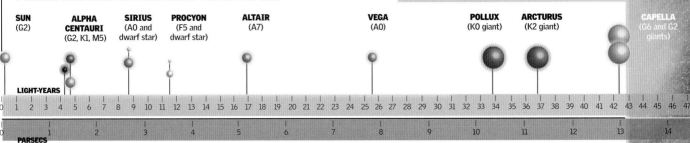

| SUN (G2) | ALPHA CENTAURI (G2, K1, M5) | SIRIUS (A0 and dwarf star) | PROCYON (F5 and dwarf star) | ALTAIR (A7) | VEGA (A0) | POLLUX (K0 giant) | ARCTURUS (K2 giant) | CAPELLA (G6 and G2 giants) |

LIGHT-YEARS
0 1 2 3 4 5 6 7 8 9 10 11 12 13 14 15 16 17 18 19 20 21 22 23 24 25 26 27 28 29 30 31 32 33 34 35 36 37 38 39 40 41 42 43 44 45 46 47

0 1 2 3 4 5 6 7 8 9 10 11 12 13 14
PARSECS

SCORPIUS REGION

GLOBULAR CLUSTER
More than a million stars are grouped together into a spherical cluster called Omega Centauri.

OPEN CLUSTER
The Pleiades are a formation of some 400 stars that will eventually move apart.

Measuring Distance

When the Earth orbits the Sun, the closest stars appear to move in front of a background of more distant stars. The angle described by the movement of a star in a six-month period of the Earth's rotation is called its parallax. The parallax of the most distant stars are too small to measure. The closer a star is to the Earth, the greater its parallax.

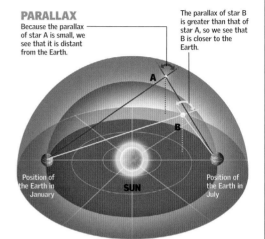

PARALLAX

Because the parallax of star A is small, we see that it is distant from the Earth.

The parallax of star B is greater than that of star A, so we see that B is closer to the Earth.

A

B

Position of the Earth in January

SUN

Position of the Earth in July

Spectral Analysis

The electromagnetic waves that make up light have different wavelengths. When light from a hot object, such as a star, is split into its different wavelengths, a band of colors, or spectrum, is obtained. Patterns of dark lines typically appear in the spectrum of a star. These patterns can be studied to determine the elements that make up the star.

Calcium   Hydrogen   Hydrogen   Sodium   Hydrogen

Wavelength longest on the red side

DOPPLER EFFECT

When a star moves toward or away from an observer, its wavelengths of light shift, a phenomenon called the Doppler effect. If the star is approaching the Earth, the dark lines in its spectrum experience a blueshift. If it moves away from the Earth, the lines experience a redshift.

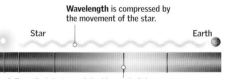

Wavelength is compressed by the movement of the star.

Star   Earth

Dark lines deviate toward the blue end of the spectrum.

BLUESHIFT of a star moving toward the Earth.

STOR
(and M1)

ALDEBARAN
(K5 giant)

ALIOTH
(A0 giant)

REGULUS
(B7 and K1)

MENKALINAN
(A2 and A2)

GACRUX
(M4 giant)

ALGOL
(B8 and K0)

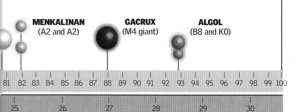

53 54 55 56 57 58 59 60 61 62 63 64 65 66 67 68 69 70 71 72 73 74 75 76 77 78 79 80 81 82 83 84 85 86 87 88 89 90 91 92 93 94 95 96 97 98 99 100

27   19   20   21   22   23   24   25   26   27   28   29   30

Stellar Evolution

Stars are born in nebulae, which are giant clouds of gas (mainly hydrogen) and dust that float in space. Stars can have a life span of millions, or even billions, of years. The biggest stars have the shortest lives, because they consume their nuclear fuel (hydrogen) at a very accelerated rate. Other stars, like the Sun, burn fuel at a slower rate and may live some 10 billion years. Many times, a star's size indicates its age. Smaller stars are the youngest, and bigger stars are approaching their end, either through cooling or by exploding as a supernova. ●

Massive star
More than 8 solar masses

Small star
Less than 8 solar masses

2. STAR
A star is finally born. It fuses hydrogen to form helium and lies along the main sequence.

1. PROTOSTAR
A protostar has a dense, gaseous core surrounded by a cloud of dust.

Nebula

A CLOUD OF GAS AND DUST collapses because of gravitational forces. In doing so it heats up and divides into smaller clouds. Each one of these clouds will form a protostar.

Life Cycle of a Star

The evolution of a star depends on its mass. The smallest ones, like the Sun, have relatively long and modest lives. Such a star begins to burn helium when its hydrogen is depleted. In this way, its external layers begin to swell until the star turns into a red giant. It ends its life as white dwarfs, eventually fading away completely, ejecting remaining outer layers, and forming a planetary nebula. A massive star, because of its higher density, can form elements heavier than helium from its nuclear reactions. In the final stage of its life, its core collapses and the star explodes. All that remains is a hyperdense remnant, a neutron star. The most massive stars end by forming black holes.

1. PROTOSTAR
A protostar is formed by the separation of gas and dust. Gravitational effects cause its core to rotate.

2. STAR The star shines and slowly consumes its hydrogen. It begins to fuse helium as its size increases.

3. **RED SUPERGIANT**
The star swells and heats up. Through nuclear reactions, a heavy core of iron is formed.

4. **SUPERNOVA** When the star can no longer fuse any more elements, its core collapses, causing a strong emission of energy.

5. **BLACK HOLE** If the star's initial mass is 20 solar masses or more, its nucleus is denser and it turns into a black hole, whose gravitational force is extremely strong.

5. **NEUTRON STAR**
If the star's initial mass is between eight and 20 solar masses, it ends up as a neutron star.

6. **BLACK DWARF**
If a white dwarf fades out completely, it becomes a black dwarf.

3. **RED GIANT** The star continues to expand, but its mass remains constant and its core heats up. When the star's helium is depleted, it fuses carbon and oxygen.

5. **WHITE DWARF**
The star remains surrounded by gases and is dim.

4. **PLANETARY NEBULA** When the star's fuel is depleted, its core condenses, and its outer layers detach, expelling gases in an expanding shell of gases.

95% of stars end their lives as white dwarfs. Other (larger) stars explode as supernovae, illuminating galaxies for weeks, although their brightness is often obscured by the gases and dust.

Red, Danger, and Death

When a star exhausts its hydrogen, it begins to die. The helium that now makes up the star's core begins to undergo nuclear reactions, and the star remains bright. When the star's helium is depleted, fusion of carbon and oxygen begins, which causes the star's core to contract. The star continues to live, though its surface layers begin to expand and cool as the star turns into a red giant. Stars similar to the Sun (solar-type stars) follow this process. After billions of years, they end up as white dwarfs. When they are fully extinguished, they will be black dwarfs, invisible in space. ●

LIFE CYCLE OF A STAR

Red giant

Red Giant

All stars go through a red-giant stage. Depending on a star's mass, it may collapse or it may simply die enveloped in gaseous layers. The core of a red giant is 10 times smaller than it was originally since it shrinks from a lack of hydrogen. A supergiant star (one with an initial mass greater than eight solar masses) lives a much shorter life. Because of the high density attained by its core, it eventually collapses in on itself and explodes.

DIAMETER

Red supergiant. Placed at the center of the solar system, it would swallow up Mars and Jupiter.

Red giant. Placed at the center of the solar system, it could reach only the nearer planets, such as Mercury, Venus, and the Earth.

- Sun
- Mercury's orbit
- Venus's orbit
- Earth's orbit
- Mars's orbit
- Jupiter's orbit
- Saturn's orbit

SPECTACULAR DIMENSIONS

On leaving the main sequence, the star enlarges to 200 times the size of the Sun. When the star begins to burn helium, its size decreases to between 10 and 100 times the size of the Sun. The star then remains stable until it becomes a white dwarf.

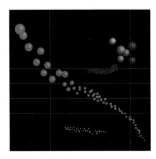

HERTZSPRUNG-RUSSELL
When the star exhausts its hydrogen, it leaves the main sequence and burns helium as a red giant (or a supergiant). The smallest stars take billions of years to leave the main sequences. The color of a red giant is caused by its relatively cool surface temperature of 3,600° F (2,000° C).

Convection Cells

Convection cells carry heat toward the surface of a star. The ascending currents of gas eventually reach the surface of the star, carrying with them a few elements that formed in the star's core.

REGION OF THE CORE

1 HYDROGEN
Hydrogen continues undergoing nuclear fusion in the exterior of the core even when the inner core has run out of hydrogen.

2 HELIUM
Helium is produced by the fusion of hydrogen during the main sequence.

3 CARBON AND OXYGEN
Carbon and oxygen are produced by the fusion of helium within the core of the red giant.

4 TEMPERATURE
As the helium undergoes fusion, the temperature of the core reaches millions of degrees Fahrenheit (millions of degrees Celsius).

SUN 1%

The scale of the diameter of the Sun to the diameter of a typical red giant.

White Dwarf

After going through the red-giant stage, a solar-type star loses its outer layers, giving rise to a planetary nebula. In its center remains a white dwarf—a relatively small, very hot (360,000° F [200,000° C]), dense star. After cooling for millions of years, it shuts down completely and becomes a black dwarf.

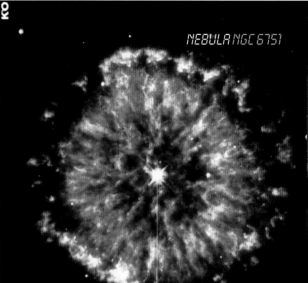

NEBULA NGC 6751

WHITE DWARF
After the nuclear reaction in the star's core ceases, the star ejects its outer layers, which then form a planetary nebula.

Hot Spots

Hot spots appear when large jets of incandescent gas reach the star's surface. They can be detected on the surface of red giants.

Dust Grains

Dust grains condense in the star's outer atmosphere and later disperse in the form of stellar winds. The dust acquires a dark appearance and is swept into interstellar space, where new generations of stars will form. The outer layer of the star may extend across several light-years of interstellar space.

HERTZSPRUNG-RUSSELL
When a white dwarf leaves the red-giant stage, it occupies the lower-left corner of the H-R diagram. Its temperature may be double that of a typical red giant. A massive white dwarf can collapse in on itself and end its life as a neutron star.

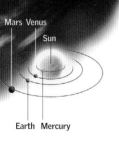

Mars Venus
Sun
Earth Mercury

Mars Venus
Sun
Earth Mercury

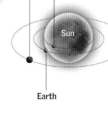

Mars Venus
Sun
Earth

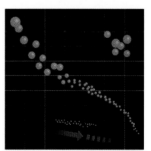

Earth

RED GIANT
The radius of the Sun reaches the Earth's orbit.

THE FUTURE OF THE SUN

Like any typical star, the Sun burns hydrogen during its main sequence. After taking approximately five billion years to exhaust its supply of hydrogen, it will begin its transformation into a red giant, doubling in brightness and expanding until it swallows Mercury. At its maximum size, it may even envelop the Earth. Once it has stabilized, it will continue as a red giant for two billion years and then become a white dwarf.

Gas Shells

When a small star dies, all that remains is an expanding gas shell known as a planetary nebula, which has nothing to do with the planets. In general, planetary nebulae are symmetrical or spherical objects. Although it has not been possible to determine why they exist in such diversity, the reason may be related to the effects of the magnetic field of the dying central star. Viewed through a telescope, several nebulae can be seen to contain a central dwarf star, a mere remnant of its precursor star. ●

LIFE CYCLE OF A STAR

Planetary nebula

BUTTERFLY

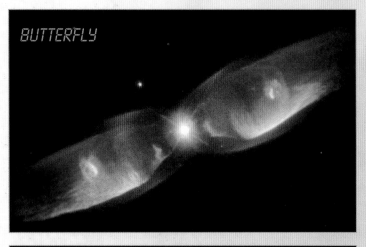

SPIROGRAPH

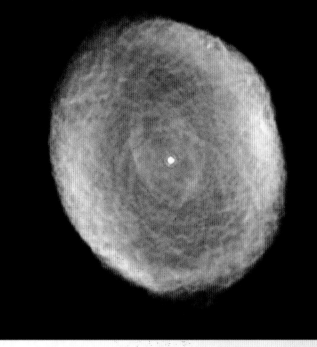

◀ **M2-9**
The Butterfly Nebula contains a star in addition to a white dwarf. Each orbits the other inside a gas disk that is 10 times larger than Pluto's orbit. The Butterfly Nebula is located 2,100 light-years from Earth.

TWICE THE TEMPERATURE OF THE SUN
is reached at the surface of a white dwarf, causing it to appear white even though its luminosity is a thousand times less than that of the Sun.

◀ **IC 418**
The Spirograph Nebula has a hot, luminous core that excites nearby atoms, causing them to glow. The Spirograph Nebula is about 0.1 light-year wide and is located 2,000 light-years from Earth.

CHANDRASEKHAR LIMIT

The astrophysicist Subrahmanyan Chandrasekhar, winner of the Nobel Prize for Physics in 1983, calculated the maximum mass a star could have so that it would not eventually collapse on itself. If a star's mass exceeds this limit, the star will eventually explode in a supernova.

1.44 SOLAR MASSES
is the limit Chandrasekhar obtained. In excess of this value, a dwarf star cannot support its own gravity and collapses.

White Dwarf

The remains of the red giant, in which the fusion of carbon and oxygen has ceased, lie at the center of the nebula. The star slowly cools and fades.

NGC 6542 CAT'S EYE

HELIX

Concentric circles

of gas, resembling the inside of an onion, form a multilayered structure around the white dwarf. Each layer has a mass greater than the combined mass of all the planets in the solar system.

3 tons

is the weight of a single tablespoon of a white dwarf. A white dwarf is very massive in spite of the fact that its diameter of 9,300 miles (or 15,000 km) is comparable to the Earth's.

NGC 7293 ▶

The Helix is a planetary nebula that was created at the end of the life of a solar-type star. It is 650 light-years from the Earth and is located in the constellation Aquarius.

HOURGLASS

MYCN 18 ▶

The two rings of colored gas form the silhouette of this hourglass-shaped nebula. The red in the photograph corresponds to nitrogen, and the green corresponds to hydrogen. This nebula is 8,000 light-years from the Earth.

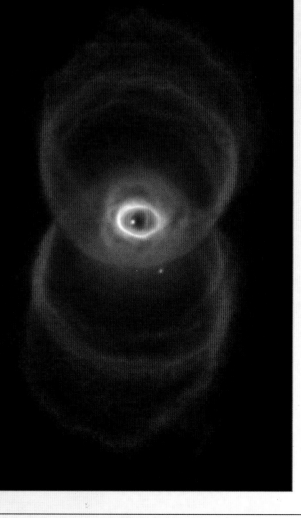

Hydrogen

The continuously expanding masses of gas surrounding the star contain mostly hydrogen, with helium and lesser amounts of oxygen, nitrogen, and other elements.

LARGER DIAMETER
Less massive white dwarf

SMALLER DIAMETER
More massive white dwarf

▲ DENSITY OF A WHITE DWARF

The density of a white dwarf is a million times greater than the density of water. In other words, each cubic meter of a white dwarf star weighs a million tons.

The mass of a star is indirectly proportional to its diameter. A white dwarf with a diameter 100 times smaller than the Sun has a mass 70 times greater.

Supernovae

A supernova is an extraordinary explosion of a giant star at the end of its life, accompanied by a sudden increase in brightness and the release of a great amount of energy. In 10 seconds, a supernova releases 100 times more energy than the Sun will release in its entire life. After the explosion of the star that gives rise to a supernova, the gaseous remnant expands and shines for millions of years. It is estimated that, in our Milky Way galaxy, two supernovae occur per century. ●

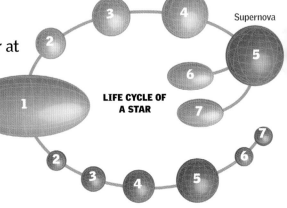

Supernova

LIFE CYCLE OF A STAR

◄ **FEBRUARY 22, 1987**
This star is in its last moments of life. Because it is very massive, it will end its life in an explosion. The galaxy exhibits only its usual luminosity.

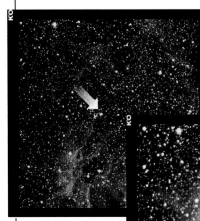

FEBRUARY 23, 1987 ►
After the supernova explosion, increased brightness is observed in the region near the star.

BEFORE AND AFTER
The image at left shows a sector of the Large Magellanic Cloud, an irregular galaxy located 170,000 light-years from the Earth, depicted before the explosion of supernova 1987A. The image at right shows the supernova.

The Twilight of a Star

The explosion that marks the end of a supergiant's life occurs because the star's extremely heavy core has become incapable of supporting its own gravity any longer. In the absence of fusion in its interior, the star falls in upon itself, expelling its remaining gases, which will expand and shine for hundreds—or even thousands—of years. The explosion of the star injects new material into interstellar space and contributes heavy atoms that can give rise to new generations of stars.

Core

A star's core can be seen to be separated into distinct layers that correspond to the different elements created during nuclear fusion. The last element created before the star's collapse is iron.

FUSION
The nuclear reactions in a dying star occur at a faster rate than they do in a red giant.

Supergiant

The diameter of the star may increase to more than 1,000 times that of the Sun. Through nuclear fusion, the star can produce elements even heavier than carbon and oxygen.

DENSE CORE

Other Elements

When a star's iron core increases in density to 1.44 solar masses, the star can no longer support its own weight and it collapses upon itself. The resulting explosion causes the formation of elements that are heavier than iron, such as gold and uranium.

Explosion

The star's life ends in an immense explosion. During the weeks following the explosion, great quantities of energy are radiated that are sometimes greater than the energy emitted by the star's parent galaxy. A supernova may illuminate its galaxy for weeks.

THE END
Either a neutron star or a black hole may form depending on the initial mass of the star that has died.

KO

SUPERMASSIVE
The mass of Eta Carinae is 100 times greater than that of the Sun. Astronomers believe that Eta Carinae is about to explode, but no one knows when.

ETA CARINAE

EPT▷12

GAS AND DUST
Gas and dust that have accumulated in the two visible lobes absorb the blue light and ultraviolet rays emitted from its center.

EPT▷11

CRAB NEBULA

GASEOUS FILAMENTS
Gaseous filaments are ejected by the supernova at 620 miles (1,000 km) per second.

Stellar Remnant

When the star explodes as a supernova, it leaves as a legacy in space the heavy elements (such as carbon, oxygen, and iron) that were in the star's nucleus before its collapse. The Crab Nebula (M1) was created by a supernova seen in 1054 by Chinese astronomers. The Crab Nebula is located 6.5 light-years from Earth and has a diameter of six light-years. The star that gave rise to the Crab Nebula may have had an initial mass close to 10 solar masses. In 1969, a pulsar radiating X-rays and rotating 33 times per second was discovered at the center of the nebula, making the Crab Nebula a very powerful source of radiation.

The Final Darkness

The last stage in the evolution of a star's core is its transformation into a very dense, compact stellar body. Its particulars depend upon the amount of mass involved in its collapse. The largest stars become black holes, their density so great that their gravitational forces capture even light. The only way to detect these dead stars is by searching for the effects of their gravitation. ●

LIFE CYCLE OF A STAR

Black hole

Neutron star

Discovery of Black Holes

The only way of detecting the presence of a black hole in space is by its effect on neighboring stars. Since the gravitational force exerted by a black hole is so powerful, the gases of nearby stars are absorbed at great speed, spiraling toward the black hole and forming a structure called an accretion disk. The friction of the gases heats them until they shine brightly. The hottest parts of the accretion disk may reach 100,000,000° C and are a source of

X-rays. The black hole, by exerting such powerful gravitational force, attracts everything that passes close to it, letting nothing escape. Since even light is not exempt from this phenomenon, black holes are opaque and invisible to even the most advanced telescopes. Some astronomers believe that supermassive black holes might have a mass of millions, or even billions, of solar masses.

Accretion Disk

An accretion disk is a gaseous accumulation of matter that the black hole draws from nearby stars. In the regions of the disk very close to the black hole, X-rays are emitted. The gas that accumulates rotates at very high speeds. When the gases from other stars collide with the disk, they create bright, hot spots.

X-RAYS
As gases enter the black hole, they are heated and emit X-rays.

LIGHT RAYS

Total escape
Rays of light that pass far from the center of a black hole continue unaffected.

Close to the limit
Since the rays of light have not crossed the event horizon, they still retain their brightness.

Darkness
Rays of light that pass close to the core of a black hole are trapped.

CROSS SECTION

ACCRETION DISK

X-RAYS

HOT GASES

BLACK HOLE

Bright ga

Since the accretion disk is fed b spinning at high speed, i intensely in the region closest to but at its edges is colder and

Neutron Star

When a star's initial mass is between 10 and 20 solar masses, its final mass will be larger than the mass of the Sun. Despite losing great quantities of matter during nuclear reactions, the star finishes with a very dense core. Because of its intense magnetic and gravitational fields, a neutron star can end up as a pulsar. A pulsar is a rapidly spinning neutron star that gives off a beam of radio waves or other radiation. As the beam sweeps around the object, the radiation is observed in very regular pulses.

Strong Gravitational Attraction

The gravitational force of the black hole attracts gases from a neighboring star. This gas forms a large spiral that swirls faster and faster as it gets closer to the black hole. The gravitation field that it generates is so strong that it traps objects that pass close to it.

1

RED GIANT
A red giant leaves the main sequence. Its diameter is 100 times greater than the Sun's.

2

SUPERGIANT
A supergiant grows and rapidly fuses heavier chemical elements, forming carbon, oxygen, and finally iron.

3

EXPLOSION
The star's iron core collapses. Protons and electrons annihilate each other and form neutrons.

LOSS OF MASS
Toward the end of its life, a neutron star loses more than 90 percent of its initial mass.

4

DENSE CORE
The core's exact composition is presently unknown. Most of its interacting particles are neutrons.

1 billion

tons is what one tablespoon of a neutron star would weigh. Its small diameter causes the star to have a compact, dense core accompanied by intense gravitational effects.

CURVED SPACE

The theory of relativity suggests that gravity is not a force but a distortion of space. This distortion creates a gravitational well, the depth of which depends on the mass of the object. Objects are attracted to other objects through the curvature of space.

1 **THE SUN** forms a shallow gravitational well.

2 **A WHITE DWARF** generates a deeper gravitational well, drawing in objects at a higher speed.

3 **A NEUTRON STAR** attracts objects at speeds approaching half the speed of light. The gravitational well is even more pronounced.

4 **BLACK HOLE**
The objects that approach the black hole too closely are swallowed by it. The black hole's gravitational well is infinite and traps matter and light forever. The event horizon describes the limit of what is, and is not, absorbed. Any object that crosses the event horizon follows a spiral path into the gravitational well. Some scientists believe in the existence of so-called wormholes—antigravity tunnels, through which travel across the universe is hypothesized to be possible. By taking advantage of the curvature of space, scientists think it could be possible to travel from the Earth to the Moon in a matter of seconds.

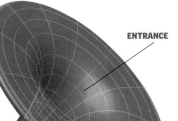

ENTRANCE

EXIT

WORMHOLE

Pulsars

The first pulsar (a neutron star radiating radio waves) was discovered in 1967. Pulsars rotate approximately 30 times per second and have very intense magnetic fields. Pulsars emit radio waves from their two magnetic poles when they rotate. If a pulsar absorbs gas from a neighboring star, a hot spot that radiates X-rays is produced on the pulsar's surface.

STRUCTURE OF A PULSAR

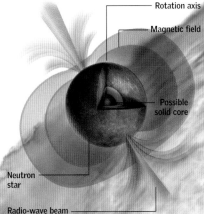

Rotation axis

Magnetic field

Possible solid core

Neutron star

Radio-wave beam

Devouring gas from a supergiant

Located within a binary system, the pulsar can follow the same process as a black hole. The pulsar's gravitational force causes it to absorb the gas of smaller, neighboring stars, heating up the pulsar's surface and causing it to emit X-rays.

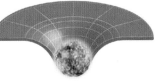

Anatomy of Galaxies

Galaxies are rotating groups of stars, gas, and dust. More than 200 years ago, philosopher Immanuel Kant postulated that nebulae were island-universes of distant stars. Even though astronomers now know that galaxies are held together by gravitational force, they have not been able to decipher what reasons might be behind galaxies' many shapes. The various types of galaxies range from ovals of old stars to spirals with arms of young stars and bright gases. The center of a galaxy has the greatest accumulation of stars. The Milky Way Galaxy is now known to be so big that rays of light, which travel at 186,000 miles (300,000 km) per second, take 100,000 years to cross from one end to the other. ●

Star Cities

➤ The first galaxies formed 100 million years after the big bang. Billions of these great conglomerates of stars can be found throughout space. The two most important discoveries concerning galaxies are attributed to the astronomer Edwin Hubble. In 1926, he pointed out that the spots, or patches, of light visible in the night sky were actually distant galaxies. Hubble's discovery put an end to the view held by astronomers at the time that the Milky Way constituted the universe. In 1929, as a result of various observations of the spectrum of light radiated by the stars in the galaxies, Hubble noted that the light from the galaxies showed a redshift (Doppler effect). This effect indicated that the galaxies were moving away from the Milky Way Galaxy. Hubble concluded that the

COLLISION

300 million light-years from the Earth, these two colliding galaxies form a pair. Together they are called "The Mice" for the large tail of stars emanating from each galaxy. With time, these galaxies will fuse into a single, larger one. It is believed that in the future the universe will consist of a few giant stars.

NGC 4676

1

1.2 BILLION YEARS ago, the Antennae (NGC 4038 and NGC 4039) were two separate spiral galaxies.

2

300 MILLION YEARS later, the galaxies collided at great speed.

MILKY WAY

Seen from its side, the Milky Way looks like a flattened disk, swollen at the center. Around the disk is a spherical region, called a halo, containing dark matter and globular clusters of stars. From June to September, the Milky Way is especially bright, something that would make it more visible viewed from above than from the side.

CLASSIFYING GALAXIES ACCORDING TO HUBBLE

NGC 6205 HERCULES

EPT▷12

EPT▷11

ELLIPTICAL
These galaxies are elliptical in shape and have little dust and gas. Their masses fall within a wide range.

SPIRAL
In a spiral galaxy, a nucleus of old stars is surrounded by a flat disk of stars and two or more spiral arms.

IRREGULAR
Irregular galaxies have no defined shape and cannot be classified. They contain a large amount of gases and dust clouds.

SUBCLASSIFICATIONS

E0 E3 E5 E7

Sa Sb Sc

SUBCLASSIFICATIONS
Galaxies are subdivided into different categories according to their tendency toward round shape (in the case of elliptical galaxies), as well as by the presence of an axis and the length of their arms (in the case of spiral and barred spiral galaxies). An E0 galaxy is elliptical but almost circular, and an E7 galaxy is a flattened oval. An Sa galaxy has a large central axis and coiled arms, and an Sc galaxy has a thinner axis and more extended arms.

Galactic Clusters

Galaxies are objects that tend to form groups or clusters. Acting in response to gravitational force, they can form clusters of galaxies of anywhere from two to thousands of galaxies. These clusters have various shapes and are thought to expand when they join together. The Hercules cluster, shown here, was discovered by Edmond Halley in 1714 and is located approximately 25,100 light-years from Earth. Each dot represents a galaxy that includes billions of stars.

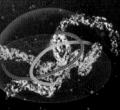

universe is expanding. But the expansion of the universe does not imply that galaxies are growing in numbers. On the contrary, galaxies can collide and merge. When two galaxies collide, they can distort each other in various ways. Over time, there are fewer and fewer galaxies. Some galaxies exhibit very peculiar shapes. The Sombrero Galaxy, shown in the center of the page, has a bright white core surrounded by thin spiral arms.

3
300 MILLION YEARS go by until the collision takes place and the shapes of the galaxies are distorted.

4
300 MILLION YEARS later, the stars in the spiral arms are expelled from both galaxies.

5
NOW two jets of expelled stars stretch far from the original galaxies.

Active Galaxies

A small number of galaxies differ from the rest by emitting high amounts of energy. The energy emission might be caused by the presence of black holes in its core that were formed through the gravitational collapse accompanying the death of supermassive stars. During their first billion years, the galaxies might have accumulated surrounding gaseous disks with their corresponding emissions of radiation. It is possible that the cores of the first galaxies are the quasars that are now observed at very great distances. ●

GAS

As two jets are expelled from the core, radio waves are emitted. If the waves collide with clouds of intergalactic gas, they swell and form gigantic clouds that can emit radio waves or X-rays.

Energetic Activity

Astronomers believe that active galaxies are a direct legacy from the beginning of the universe. After the big bang, these galaxies would have retained very energetic levels of radiation. Quasars, the brightest and most ancient objects in the universe, make up the core of this type of galaxy. In some cases, they emit X-rays or radio waves. The existence of this high-energy activity helps support the theory that galaxies could be born from a supermassive black hole with a quasar that became inactive as stars formed and it was left without gas to feed it. This process of formation might be common to many galaxies. Today quasars represent the limit of what it is possible to see, even with specialized telescopes. Quasars are small, dense, and bright.

CENTRAL RING

The core of an active galaxy is obscured by a ring of dust and gas that is dark on the outside and bright within. It is a powerful source of energy.

① The Force of Gravity

Gravitational force begins to unite vast quantities of hot, gaseous clouds. The clouds attract one another and collide, forming stars. A large amount of gas accumulates at the center of the galaxy, intensifying gravitational forces until a massive black hole comes into being in the galaxy's core.

② The Quasar in the Core

The quasar in the core ejects two jets of particles that reach speeds approaching the speed of light. The quasar stage is thought to have been the most violent stage in the formation of galaxies. The gases and stars arising from the jets are introduced as spirals into the black hole, forming a type of accretion disk known as a quasar.

③ Black Hole

A black hole swallows the gas that begins to surround it. A hot, gaseous spiral forms, emitting high-speed jets. The magnetic field pours charged particles into the region around the black hole, and the exterior of the disk absorbs interstellar gas.

CLASSIFICATION

The classification of an active galaxy depends upon its distance from Earth and the perspective from which it is seen. Quasars, radio galaxies, and blazars are members of the same family of objects and differ only in the way they are perceived.

QUASARS The most powerful objects in the universe, quasars are so distant from Earth that they appear to us as diffuse stars. They are the bright cores of remote galaxies.

RADIO GALAXIES Radio galaxies are the largest objects in the universe. Jets of gases come out from their centers that extend thousands of light-years. The cores of radio galaxies cannot be seen.

BLAZARS Blazars may be active galaxies with jets of gas that are aimed directly toward Earth. The brightness of a blazar varies from day to day.

3 The strong gravitational force of the disk attracts and destroys stars.

2 As the gases move inward, their temperature increases.

4 The center of the black hole radiates charged particles.

100
MILLION DEGREES
Celsius is the temperature that the core of a black hole can reach.

ACCRETION DISK
Formed by interstellar gas and star remnants, the accretion disk can radiate X-rays because of the extreme temperature of its center.

PARTICLES
ejected from the black hole have intense magnetic fields. The jets of particles travel at speeds approaching the speed of light when they leave the core.

Galaxy Formation

A theory of galaxy formation associated with active galaxies holds that many galaxies, possibly including the Milky Way, were formed from the gradual calming of a quasar at their core. As the surrounding gases consolidated in the formation of stars, the quasars, having no more gases to absorb, lost their energetic fury and became inactive. According to this theory, there is a natural progression from quasars to active galaxies to the common galaxies of today. In 1994, astronomers studying the center of the Milky Way discovered a region that may contain a black hole and could be left over from early galactic activity.

GASEOUS CLOUDS
Gaseous clouds appeared from the gravitational collapse of immense masses of gas during the early stages of the universe. Later, in the clouds' interior, stars began to form.

INCREASING GRAVITY

1 Dark clouds of gas and dust on the outer edge of a black hole are gradually swallowed up.

Stable Galaxy

Nine billion years after its formation, with a supermassive black hole at its core, the galaxy drastically slows its energetic activity, forming a low-energy core. The stabilization of the galaxy allowed the formation of stars and other heavenly bodies.

Stellar Metropolis

For a long time, our galaxy (called the Milky Way because of its resemblance to a stream of milk in the night sky) was a true enigma. It was Galileo Galilei who, in 1610, first pointed a telescope at the Milky Way and saw that the weak whitish strip was composed of thousands and thousands of stars that appeared to almost touch each other. Little by little, astronomers began to realize that all these stars, like our own Sun, were part of the enormous ensemble—the galaxy that is our stellar metropolis. ●

Large
Magellanic Cloud

MILKY WAY

Small
Magellanic
Cloud

Triangle
Galaxy

Andromeda
Galaxy

Structure of the Milky Way

The Milky Way, containing more than 100 billion stars, has two spiral arms rotating around its core. The Sagittarius arm, located between the Orion arm and the center of the Milky Way, holds one of the most luminous stars in the galaxy, Eta Carinae. The Perseus arm, the main outer arm of the Milky Way, contains young stars and nebulae. The Orion arm, extending between Perseus and Sagittarius, houses the solar system within its inner border. The Orion arm of the Milky Way is a veritable star factory, where gaseous interstellar material can give birth to billions of stars. Remnants of stars can also be found within it.

ROTATION

The speeds of the rotation of the various parts of the Milky Way vary according to those parts' distances from the core of the galaxy. The greatest number of stars is concentrated in the region between the Milky Way's core and its border. Here the speed of rotation is much greater because of the attraction that the objects in this region feel from the billions of stars within it.

120 miles per hour (200 km/h)

140 miles per hour (220 km/h)

150 miles per hour (240 km/h)

155 miles per hour (250 km/h)

0°

360°

30°

Central
protuberance

60°

90°

3KPC ARM

NORMA ARM

PERSEUS ARM

ORION ARM

SAGITTARIUS ARM

120°

Eta
Carinae

Eagle
Nebula

SOLAR SYSTEM

Orion
Nebula

6,000 light-years

Cassiopeia A

Crab
Nebula

150°

180°

Central Region

Because the Milky Way is full of clouds of dust and rock particles, its center cannot be seen from outside the galaxy. The Milky Way's center can be seen only through telescopes that record infrared light, radio waves, or X-rays, which can pass through the material that blocks visible light. The central axis of the Milky Way contains ancient stars, some 14 billion years old, and exhibits intense activity within its interior, where two clouds of hot gas have been found: Sagittarius A and B. In the central region, but outside the core, a giant dark cloud contains 70 different types of molecules. These gas clouds are associated with violent activity in the center of our galaxy and contain the heart of the Milky Way within their depths. In general, the stars in this region are cold and range in color from red to orange.

SAGITTARIUS B2
The largest dark cloud in the central region of the Milky Way, Sagittarius B2 contains enough alcohol to cover the entire Earth.

MAGNETISM
The center of the Milky Way is surrounded by strong magnetic fields, perhaps from a rotating black hole.

HOT GASES
The hot gases originating from the surface of the central region may be the result of violent explosions in the accretion disk.

BRIGHT STARS
Bright stars are born from gas that is not absorbed by the black hole. Most of them are young.

BLACK HOLE
Many astronomers believe that a black hole occupies the center of the Milky Way. Its strong gravitational force would trap gases in orbit around it.

GASES SWIRL
outward because of forces in the Sagittarius A region. Because the gas rotates at high speed but remains concentrated, it could be trapped by gravitational forces exerted by a black hole.

The Exact Center

The core of the Milky Way galaxy is marked by very intense radio-wave activity that might be produced by an accretion disk made up of incandescent gas surrounding a massive black hole. The region of Sagittarius A, discovered in 1994, is a gas ring that rotates at very high speed, swirling within several light-years of the center of the galaxy. The speed of its rotation is an indication of the powerful gravitational force exerted from the center of the Milky Way, a force stronger than would be produced by the stars located in the region. The hot, blue stars that shine in the center of the Milky Way may have been born from gas not yet absorbed by the black hole.

A Diverse Galaxy

The brightest portion of the Milky Way that appears in photographs taken with optical lenses (using visible light) is in the constellation Sagittarius, which appears to lie in the direction of the center of the Milky Way. The bright band in the nighttime sky is made up of stars so numerous that it is almost impossible to count them. In some cases, stars are obscured by dense dust clouds that make some regions of the Milky Way seem truly dark. The objects that can be found in the Milky Way are not all of one type. Some, such as those known as the halo population, are old and are distributed within a sphere around the galaxy. Other objects form a more flattened structure called the disk population. In the spiral arm population, we find the youngest objects in the Milky Way. In these arms, gas and interstellar dust abound.

CARINA ARM

270°

OUTER RING
A ring of dark clouds of dust and molecules that is expanding as a result of a giant explosion. It is suspected that a small object in the central region of the Milky Way might be its source.

240°

OUTER ARM

210°

100,000
LIGHT-YEARS
The diameter of the Milky Way is large in comparison with other galaxies but not gigantic.

THE MILKY WAY IN VISIBLE LIGHT

THE CONSTELLATION SAGITTARIUS
Close to the center of the Milky Way, Sagittarius shines intensely.

DARK REGIONS
Dark regions are produced by dense clouds that obscure the light of stars.

SECTORS
Many different sectors make up the Milky Way.

STARS
So many stars compose the Milky Way that it is impossible for us to distinguish them all.

The Solar System

A mong the millions and millions of stars that form the Milky Way galaxy, there is a medium-sized one located in one of the galaxy's arms—the Sun. To ancient peoples, the Sun was a god; to us, it is the central source of energy that generates heat, helping life exist. This star, together with the planets and other bodies that spin in orbits around it, make up the solar system, which formed about 4.6 billion years ago. The planets that rotate around it do not produce their own light. Instead, they reflect sunlight. After the Earth, Mars is the most explored planet. Here we see a photo of Olympus Mons, the largest volcano in the entire solar system. It is almost two-and-a-half times as high as the tallest peak on the Earth, Mount Everest. ●

Attracted by a Star

Planets and their satellites, asteroids and other rocky objects, and an incalculable number of cometlike objects, some more than 1 trillion miles (1.6 trillion km) from the Sun, make up the solar system. In the 17th century, astronomer Johannes Kepler proposed a model to interpret the dynamic properties of the bodies of the solar system. According to this interpretation, the planets complete elliptical trajectories, called orbits, around the Sun. In every case, the movement is produced by the influence of the gravitational field of the Sun. Today, as part of a rapidly developing field of astronomy, it is known that planet or planetlike bodies also orbit other stars. ●

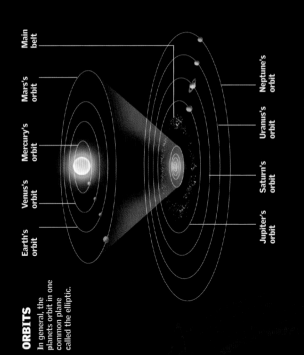

ORBITS
In general, the planets orbit in one common plane called the elliptic.

Earth's orbit

Venus's orbit

Mercury's orbit

Mars's orbit

Main belt

Jupiter's orbit

Saturn's orbit

Uranus's orbit

Neptune's orbit

The rotation of most planets around their own axes is in counterclockwise direction. Venus and Uranus, however, revolve clockwise.

Outer Planets

Planets located outside the asteroid belt. They are enormous gas spheres with small solid cores. They have very low temperatures because of their great distance from the Sun. The presence of ring systems is exclusive to these planets. The greatest of them is Jupiter: 1,300 Earths could fit inside of it. Its mass is 2.5 times as great as that of the rest of the planets combined.

NEPTUNE
DIAMETER   30,775 MILES (49,528 KM)
MOONS   13

Triton   Proteus   Nereid

URANUS
DIAMETER   31,763 MILES (51,118 KM)
MOONS   27

Titania   Oberon   Umbriel   Ariel   Miranda   Puck

SATURN
DIAMETER   74,898 MILES (120,536 KM)
MOONS   50+

Titan   Rhea   Iapetus   Tethys

BUILDING PLANETS

Early ideas suggested that the planets formed gradually, beginning with the binding of hot dust particles. Today scientists suggest that the planets originated from the collision and melding of larger-sized bodies called planetesimals.

1 **ORIGIN**
Remains from the formation of the Sun created a disk of gas and dust around it, from which the planetesimals formed.

2 **COLLISION**
Through collisions among themselves, planetesimals of different sizes joined together to become more massive objects.

3 **HEAT**
The collisions produced a large amount of heat that accumulated in the interior of the planets, according to their distance from the Sun.

SOLAR GRAVITY

The gravitational pull of the Sun upon the planets not only keeps them inside the solar system but also influences the speed with which they revolve in their orbits around the Sun. Those closest to the Sun revolve in their orbits much faster than those farther from it.

JUPITER

DIAMETER 88,846 MILES (142,984 KM)

MOONS 60+

Ganymede   Callisto   Io   Europa

Asteroid Belt

The border between the outer and inner planets is marked by millions of rocky fragments of various sizes that form a band called the asteroid belt. Their orbits are influenced by the gravitational pull exerted on them by the giant planet Jupiter. This effect also keeps them from merging and forming a planet.

Inner Planets

Planets located inside the asteroid belt. They are solid bodies in which internal geologic phenomena, such as volcanism, which can modify their surfaces, are produced. Almost all of them have an appreciable atmosphere of some degree of thickness, according to individual circumstances, which plays a key role in the surface temperatures of each planet.

MARS
DIAMETER 4,217 MILES (6,786 KM)
MOONS 2

Phobos Deimos

EARTH
DIAMETER 7926 MILES (12,756 KM)
MOONS 1

MOON

MERCURY
DIAMETER 3,031 MILES (4,878 KM)
MOONS 0

VENUS
DIAMETER 7,520 MILES (12,103 KM)
MOONS 0

S U N

A Very Warm Heart

The Sun at the center of the solar system is a source of light and heat. This energy is produced by the fusion of atomic hydrogen nuclei, which generate helium nuclei. The energy that emanates from the Sun travels through space and initially encounters the bodies that populate the solar system. The Sun shines thanks to thermonuclear fusion, and it will continue to shine until its supply of hydrogen runs out in about six or seven billion years. ●

Very Gassy

The Sun is a giant ball of gases with very high density and temperature. Its main components are hydrogen (90%) and helium (9%). The balance of its mass is made up of trace elements, such as carbon, nitrogen, and oxygen, among others. Because of the conditions of extreme temperature and pressure on the Sun, these elements are in a plasma state.

CHARACTERISTICS

CONVENTIONAL
PLANET
SYMBOL

ESSENTIAL DATA

Average distance from Earth	93 million miles (150 million km)
Equatorial diameter	864,000 miles (1,391,000 km)
Orbital speed	7,456 miles per second (12,000 km/s)
Mass*	332,900
Gravity*	28
Density	0.81 ounce per cubic inch (1.4 g per cu cm)
Average temperature	9,932° F (5,500° C)
Atmosphere	Dense
Moons	None

*In both cases, Earth = 1

NUCLEAR FUSION OF HYDROGEN

The extraordinary temperature of the nuclear core helps the hydrogen nuclei join. Under conditions of lower energy, they repel each other, but the conditions at the center of the Sun can overcome the repulsive forces, and nuclear fusion occurs. For every four hydrogen nuclei, a series of nuclear reactions produce one helium nucleus.

CONVECTIVE ZONE

extends from the base of the photosphere down to a depth of 15 percent of the solar radius. Here energy is transported up toward the surface by gas currents (through convection).

RADIATIVE ZONE

This portion of the Sun is traversed by particles coming from the core. A proton can take a million years to cross this zone.

14,400,000° F
(8,000,000° C)

1. NUCLEAR COLLISION

Two hydrogen nuclei (two protons) collide and remain joined. One changes into a neutron, and deuterium forms, releasing a neutrino, a positron, and a lot of energy.

Proton
Positron
Neutron
Neutrino

Deuterium

Photon

2. PHOTONS

The deuterium formed collides with a proton. This collision releases one photon and gamma rays. The high-energy photon needs 30,000 years to reach the photosphere.

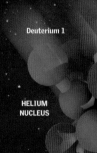

Deuterium 1

HELIUM NUCLEUS

Deuterium 2

3. HELIUM NUCLEI

The group of two protons and a neutron collides with another such group. A helium nucleus forms, and a pair of protons is released.

Proton 1

Proton 2

Surface and Atmosphere

The visible portion of the Sun is a sphere of light, or photosphere, made of boiling gases emanating from the solar core. The gas flares form plasma, which passes through this layer. Later the gas flares enter a vast gas layer called the solar atmosphere. The density of this layer decreases toward its outermost region. Above the photosphere lies the solar atmosphere—the chromosphere and the corona. The energy generated at the core moves through the surface of the photosphere and solar atmosphere for thousands of years in search of an exit into space.

SUNSPOTS
are regions of gases that are generally colder (7,232° F [4,000° C]) than the photosphere (10,112° F [5,600° C]). For that reason, they appear dark.

PENUMBRA
Peripheral region. It is the hottest and brightest part of the Sun.

UMBRA
Central region. It is the coldest and darkest part.

PHOTOSPHERE

The visible surface of the Sun, a boiling tide, is thick with gases in a plasma state. In its uppermost layer, its density decreases and its transparency increases, and the solar radiation escapes from the Sun as light. The spectrographic study of this layer has allowed scientists to confirm that the main components of the Sun are hydrogen and helium.

10,112° F
(5,600° C)

CHROMOSPHERE

Above the photosphere, and of less density, lies the chromosphere, a layer 3,110 miles (5,000 km) thick. Its temperature ranges from 8,100° F (4,500° C) to 900,000° F (500,000° C) with increasing altitude. The temperature of the corona can reach 1,800,000° F (1,000,000° C).

900,000° F
(500,000° C)

MAXIMUM TEMPERATURE OF THE CHROMOSPHERE

CORE
The core occupies only 2 percent of the total volume of the Sun, but in it is concentrated about half the total mass of the Sun. The great pressures and temperatures in the core produce thermonuclear fusion.

27,000,000° F
(15,000,000° C)

SPICULES
Vertical jets of gas that spew from the chromosphere, usually reaching 6,200 miles (10,000 km) in height. They originate in upper convection cells and can rise as high as the corona.

MACROSPICULES
This type of vertical eruption is similar to a spicule, but it usually reaches up to 25,000 miles (40,000 km) in height.

CORONA
Located above the chromosphere, it extends millions of miles into space and reaches temperatures nearing 1,800,000° F (1,000,000° C). It has some holes, or low-density regions, through which gases flow into the solar wind.

1,800,000° F
(1,000,000° C)

THE TEMPERATURE IN THE CORONA

SOLAR WIND
Consists of a flux of ions emitted by the solar atmosphere. The composition is similar to that of the corona. The Sun loses approximately 1,800 pounds (800 kg) of matter per second in the form of solar wind.

SOLAR PROMINENCES
Clouds and layers of gas from the chromosphere travel thousands of miles until they reach the corona, where the influence of magnetic fields causes them to take on the shape of an arc or wave.

SOLAR FLARES
These eruptions come out of the solar atmosphere and can interfere with radio communications on Earth.

Mercury, an Inferno

M ercury is the planet nearest to the Sun and is therefore the one that has to withstand the harshest of the Sun's effects. Due to its proximity to the Sun, Mercury moves at great speed in its solar orbit, completing an orbit every 88 days. It has almost no atmosphere, and its surface is dry and rugged, covered with craters caused by the impact of numerous meteorites; this makes it resemble the Moon. Numerous faults, formed during the cooling of the planet when it was young, are also visible on the surface. Constantly baked by its neighbor, the Sun, Mercury has an average surface temperature of 333° F (167° C). ●

A Scar-Covered Surface

➡ The surface of Mercury is very similar to that of the Moon. It is possible to find craters of varying sizes. The largest one has a diameter of some 810 miles (1,300 km). There are also hills and valleys. In 1991, radio telescopes were able to detect possible evidence of the presence of frozen water in Mercury's polar regions, information that Mariner 10 had been unable to gather. Mariner 10, the only mission sent to Mercury, flew by the planet three times between 1974 and 1975. The polar ice was found at the bottom of very deep craters, which limit the ice's exposure to the Sun's rays. The spacecraft Messenger, launched in 2004, is scheduled to orbit the planet Mercury in 2011 and is expected to provide new information about Mercury's surface and magnetic field.

CALORIS CRATER
The largest impact crater in the solar system, it has a diameter of 810 miles (1,300 km).

The crater was flooded with lava.

When the projectile that formed the crater struck, Mercury was still forming. The extensive waves that extended from the site of impact formed hills and mountains ranges.

BEETHOVEN
is the second largest crater on Mercury. It is 400 miles (643 km) in diameter. Its floor was flooded by lava and later marked by meteorite impacts.

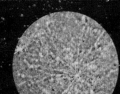

310 miles (500 Km)

2,240 miles (3,600 Km)

Missions to Mercury

➡ The space probe Mariner 10 was the first to reach Mercury. Between 1974 and 1975, the craft flew by the planet three times and came within about 200 miles (320 km) of the surface. Messenger, a space probe scheduled to study Mercury between 2008 and 2011, was launched in 2004.

Mariner 10

Messenger

The probe will pass by Mercury twice in 2008 and once again in 2009 before beginning to orbit the planet.

Composition and Magnetic Field

Like the Earth, Mercury has a magnetic field, although a much weaker one. The magnetism results from its enormous core made of solid iron. The mantle that surrounds the core is believed to be a fine layer of iron and sulfur.

29%
Sodium

22%
Hydrogen

6%
Helium

43%
Others

EXTREMELY THIN ATMOSPHERE

Mercury's atmosphere is almost nonexistent and consists of a very thin layer that cannot protect the planet either from the Sun or from meteorites. During the day, when Mercury is closer to the Sun, the planet's temperature can surpass 842° F (450° C). At night, temperatures can plummet to -297° F (-183° C).

During the night, the heat of Mercury's rocks is lost rapidly, and the planet's temperature drops.

During the day, the Sun directly heats the rock.

-297° F
(-183° C)

883° F
(473° C)

CRUST
Made of silicate rocks, Mercury's crust is similar to the crust and mantle of the Earth. It has a thickness of 310 to 370 miles (500-600 km).

CORE
Dense, large, and made of iron, its diameter may be as great as 2,240 to 2,300 miles (3,600-3,800 km).

MANTLE
Made up mostly of silica-based rocks

333° F
(167° C)

Baked by its neighbor the Sun, Mercury is the planet with the greatest thermal fluctuations in the solar system. Its average temperature is 333° F (167° C), but when it gets closer to the Sun, the temperature can climb to 842° F (450° C). At night, it drops to -297° F (-183° C).

CHARACTERISTICS

CONVENTIONAL
PLANET SYMBOL

☿

ESSENTIAL DATA

Average distance from the Sun	**36,000,000 miles (57,900,000 km)**
Solar orbit (Mercurian year)	**88 days 00 hours**
Equatorial diameter	**3,032 miles (4,880 km)**
Orbital speed	**29,75 miles per second (47.87 km/s)**
Mass*	**0.06**
Gravity*	**0.38**
Density	**3,14 ounces per cubic inch (5.43 g/cu cm)**
Average temperature	**332° F (167° C)**
Atmosphere	**Almost nonexistent**
Lunas	

* In both cases, Earth = 1

AXIS INCLINATION

0.1°

One rotation lasts 59 days.

Rotation and Orbit

Mercury rotates slowly on its axis and takes approximately 59 Earth days to complete a turn, but it only needs 88 days to travel in its orbit. To an observer in Mercury, these two combined motions would give a combined interval of 176 days between two sunrises. A person observing the sunrise from position 1 would have to wait for the planet to make two orbits around the Sun and make three rotations on its own axis before seeing the next sunrise.

ORBIT OF MERCURY AROUND THE SUN

SUN

3   2   4   1   5   6   7

Each number corresponds to a position of the Sun in the sky as seen from Mercury.

VIEW FROM MERCURY

6 Resumes its original path toward the horizon

3 Reaches the zenith (noon) and stops

4 Recedes a bit

5 Stops again

7 Decreases toward the sunset

2 Rises and increases its size

1 The Sun rises.

HORIZON OF MERCURY

Venus, Our Neighbor

Venus is the second closest planet to the Sun. Similar in size to the Earth, it has a volcanic surface, as well as a hostile atmosphere governed by the effects of carbon dioxide. Although about four billion years ago the atmospheres of the Earth and Venus were similar, the mass of Venus's atmosphere today is 100 times greater than the Earth's. Its thick clouds of sulfuric acid and dust are so dense that stars are invisible from the planet's surface. Viewed from the Earth, Venus can be bright enough to be visible during day and second only to the moon in brightness at night. Because of this, the movements of Venus were well-known by most ancient civilizations.

CHARACTERISTICS

CONVENTIONAL PLANET SYMBOL ♀

ESSENTIAL DATA

Average distance from the Sun	67,000,000 miles (108,000,000 km)
Solar orbit (Venusian year)	224 days 17 hours
Equatorial diameter	7,520 miles (12,100 km)
Orbital speed	22 miles per second (35 km/s)
Mass*	0.8
Gravity*	0.9
Density	3.03 ounces per cubic inch (5.25 g/cu cm)
Average temperature	860° F (460° C)
Atmosphere	Very thick
Moons	None

*In both cases, Earth = 1

AXIS INCLINATION

117°

Rotates on its own axis every 243 days

GREENHOUSE EFFECT

Only 20 percent of the Sun's light reaches the surface of Venus. The thick clouds of dust, sulfuric acid, and carbon dioxide that constitute Venus's atmosphere reflect the remaining light, leaving Venus in permanent darkness.

SOLAR RADIATION

Venus is kept hot by its thick atmosphere, which retains the energy of the Sun's rays.

864° F (462° C)

INFRARED RAYS
The surface of Venus radiates infrared radiation. Only 20 percent of the Sun's rays pass through Venus's thick clouds of sulfuric acid.

Composition

The overwhelming presence of carbon dioxide in the Venusian atmosphere induces a greenhouse effect, increasing the surface temperature to 864° F (462° C). Because of this, Venus is hotter than Mercury, even though Venus is farther from the Sun and reflects all but 20 percent of the Sun's light. The surface temperature of Venus is relatively constant, averaging 860° F (460° C). The atmospheric pressure on Venus is 90 times greater than that on the Earth.

ATMOSPHERE
Venus's glowing appearance is caused by the planet's thick, suffocating atmosphere, which is made up of carbon dioxide and sulfuric clouds that reflect sunlight.

50 miles (80 km)
IS THE THICKNESS OF THE ATMOSPHERE.

Carbon dioxide 97%

Nitrogen and traces of other gases 3%

MANTLE
Made of molten rock, it constitutes most of the planet. It traps the solar radiation and is between 37 and 62 miles (60 and 100 km) thick.

CORE
It is believed that Venus's core is similar to the Earth's, containing metallic elements (iron and nickel) and silicates. Venus has no magnetic field—possibly because of its slow axial rotation.

14,400° F (8,000° C)

SULFURIC ACID

Venus lacks water. A U.S. robot probe sent to Venus in 1978 found some evidence that water vapor could have existed in the atmosphere hundreds of millions of years ago, but today no trace of water remains.

CRUST
Made up of silicates, it is thicker than the Earth's crust.

VENUS'S PHASES

As Venus revolves around the Sun, its solar illumination varies as is seen from the Earth depending upon its position in relation to the Sun and the Earth. Thus Venus has phases similar to the Moon's. During its elongations, when Venus is farthest from the Sun in the sky, Venus appears at its brightest.

VENUS'S PHASES AS SEEN FROM EARTH

WAXING CRESCENT

FIRST QUARTER

WAXING GIBBOUS

WANING GIBBOUS

LAST QUARTER

WANING CRESCENT

EARTH

VENUS

SUN

THE NEW AND FULL PHASES ARE NOT VISIBLE FROM EARTH.

The surface of Venus is rocky and dry. Most of the planet is formed by volcanic plains and other, elevated regions.

3,700 miles (6,000 km)

3,700 miles (6,000 km)

Surface

The Venusian surface has not remained the same throughout its life. The current one is some 500 million years old, but the rocky landscape visible today was formed by intense volcanic activity. Volcanic rock covers 85 percent of the planet. The entire planet is crisscrossed by vast plains and enormous rivers of lava, as well as a number of mountains. The lava flows have created a great number of grooves, some of which are very wide. The brightness of Venus's surface is the result of metallic compounds.

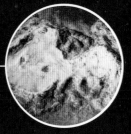

MAGELLAN
Venus was explored by the Magellan spacecraft between 1990 and 1994. The probe was equipped with a radar system to observe the surface through its dense atmosphere.

ISHTAR TERRA
One of the raised plateaus of Venus, it is similar in size to Australia and is located close to Venus's north pole. It has four main rocky mountain ranges called Maxwell Montes, Freyja Montes, Akna Montes, and Dam Montes.

APHRODITE TERRA
Larger than Ishtar Terra, it is the size of South America. Aphrodite Terra lies near the equator and consists mostly of mountainous regions to the east and west, which are separated by a low-lying region.

Red and Fascinating

M ars is the fourth planet from the Sun. Of all the planets, Mars most closely resembles the Earth. It has polar ice caps, and the tilt of its axis, period of rotation, and internal structure are similar to those of the Earth. Known as the Red Planet because of the reddish iron oxide that covers its surface, Mars has a thin atmosphere composed essentially of carbon dioxide. Mars does not have water, though it did in the past, and there is evidence some water might exist underground. Many spacecraft have been sent to explore Mars, in part because it is the planet other than Earth most likely to have developed some form of life, and it will probably be the first planet humans leave the Earth to visit. ●

Martian Orbit

Because Mars's orbit is more elliptical than that of Earth, Mars's distance from the Sun varies widely. At its perihelion, or closest approach to the Sun, Mars receives 45 percent more solar radiation than at its aphelion, or farthest point. Temperatures on Mars range from -220° F to 62° F (-140° C to 17° C).

-220° F
(-140° C)
IN WINTER

62° F
(17° C)
IN SUMMER

SUN   EARTH   MARS

Composition

Mars, a rocky planet, has an iron-rich core. Mars is almost half the size of the Earth and has a similar period of rotation, as well as clearly evident clouds, winds, and other weather phenomena. Its thin atmosphere is made up of carbon dioxide, and its red color comes from its soil, which is rich in iron oxide.

CRUST
is thin and made up of solid rock. It is 31 miles (50 km) thick.

Moons

Mars has two moons, Phobos and Deimos. Both have a lower density than Mars and are pitted with craters. Phobos has a diameter of 17 miles (27 km), and Deimos has a diameter of nine miles (15 km). Deimos orbits Mars in 30 hours at an altitude of 14,627 miles (23,540 km), and Phobos orbits Mars in eight hours at an altitude of 5,840 miles (9,400 km). Astronomers believe that the moons are asteroids that were captured by Mars's gravity.

DEIMOS

| DIAMETER | 9 MILES (15 KM) |
| DISTANCE FROM MARS | 14,627 MILES (23,540 KM) |

PHOBOS

| DIAMETER | 17 MILES (27 KM) |
| DISTANCE FROM MARS | 5,840 MILES (9,400 KM) |

Terra Sirenum

MISSIONS TO MARS

After our own Moon, Mars has been a more attractive target for exploratory missions than any other object in the solar system.

1965 MARINER 4
The first mission sent to Mars, it made only brief flyovers.

1969 MARINER 6 AND 7 studied the southern hemisphere and equator of Mars.

1971 MARINER 9 photographed the Olympus volcano for the first time.

1973 MARS 4, MARS 5, MARS 6, AND MARS 7 Russian spacecraft successfully sent to Mars

1976 VIKING 1 AND 2 searched for traces of life. They were the first spacecraft to land on Martian soil.

Surface

It is a place of geologic extremes, shaped by volcanic activity, meteorite bombardment, windstorms, and floods (though there is little or no water on Mars today). Mountains dominate the southern hemisphere, but lowlands are common in the northern hemisphere.

MANTLE
It is made of molten rock of greater density than the Earth's mantle.

CORE
Small and likely composed of iron

1,000 miles (1,700 km)

2,000 miles (3,294 km)

ATMOSPHERE
Thin and continuously thinning as solar winds diminish atmosphere

95.3%
Carbon dioxide

2.6%
Nitrogen

2.1%
Oxygen, carbon monoxide, water vapor, and other gases

Olympus Mons

Tharsis Mons

Valles Marineris

Solis Lacus

South Pole

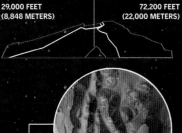

OLYMPUS MONS
This gigantic, inactive volcano is not only the largest on Mars but also in the solar system.

EVEREST
**29,000 FEET
(8,848 METERS)**

OLYMPUS
**72,200 FEET
(22,000 METERS)**

VALLES MARINERIS

The canyon system of the Valles Marineris was likely caused naturally, primarily by water erosion.

CHARACTERISTICS

CONVENTIONAL
PLANET SYMBOL

ESSENTIAL DATA

Average distance from the Sun	141,600,000 miles (227,900,000 km)
Solar orbit (Martian year)	1.88 years
Equatorial diameter	4,222 miles (6,794 km)
Orbital speed	15 miles per second (24 km/s)
Mass*	0.107
Gravity*	0.38
Density	2.27 ounces per cubic inch (3.93 g/cu cm)
Average temperature	-81° F (-63° C)
Atmosphere	Very thin
Moons	2

*In both cases, Earth = 1

AXIS INCLINATION

25.2°

One rotation lasts 1.88 years.

1997 MARS PATHFINDER was the third successful Mars landing.

1997 MARS GLOBAL SURVEYOR took more than 100,000 photos of the planet.

2001 MARS ODYSSEY mapped the mineralogy and morphology of Mars's surface.

2003 MARS EXPRESS Orbiting probe. First spacecraft sent by the European Space Agency.

2004 SPIRIT AND OPPORTUNITY surveyed many square miles of the surface.

2006 MARS RECONNAISSANCE ORBITER made a detailed study of the Martian surface while orbiting the planet.

Jupiter, Gas Giant

J upiter is the largest planet in the solar system. Its diameter is 11 times that of the Earth, and its mass is 300 times as great. Because the speed of Jupiter's rotation flattens the planet at its poles, its equatorial diameter is greater than its polar diameter. Jupiter rotates at 25,000 miles per hour (40,000 km/hr). One of the most distinctive elements of Jupiter's atmosphere is its so-called Great Red Spot, a giant high-pressure region of turbulence that has been observed from the Earth for more than 300 years. The planet is orbited by numerous satellites and has a wide, faint ring of particles. ●

Composition

Jupiter is a giant ball of hydrogen and helium that have been compressed into liquid in the planet's interior and into metallic rock in its core. Not much is known about Jupiter's core, but it is believed to be bigger than the Earth's core.

ATMOSPHERE
measures 620
miles (1,000 km).

INNER MANTLE
Surrounds the core. It is made of liquid metallic hydrogen, an element only found under hot, high-pressure conditions. The inner mantle is a soup of electrons and nuclei.

23,000 miles
(37,000 km)

17,000 miles
(27,000 km)

CHARACTERISTICS

CONVENTIONAL
PLANET SYMBOL ♃

CORE
Its size is similar to that of the Earth's core.

9,000 miles
(14,000 km)

ESSENTIAL DATA	
Average distance from the Sun	483,000,000 miles (778,000,000 km)
Solar orbit (Jovian year)	11 years 312 days
Equatorial diameter	88,700 miles (142,800 km)
Orbital speed	8 miles per second (13 km/s)
Mass*	318
Gravity*	2.36
Density	0.77 ounce per cubic inch (1.33 g/cu cm)
Average temperature	-184° F (-120° C)
Atmosphere	Very dense
Moons	More than 60

*In both cases, Earth = 1

54,000° F
(30,000° C)

AXIS INCLINATION

3.1°

One rotation lasts 9 hours and 55 minutes.

OUTER MANTLE
Made of liquid molecular hydrogen. The outer mantle merges with the atmosphere.

The Moons of Jupiter

Jupiter has more than 60 moons. Many of them have not been officially confirmed and do not even have names. Jupiter's rotation is gradually slowing because of the moons' tidal effects.

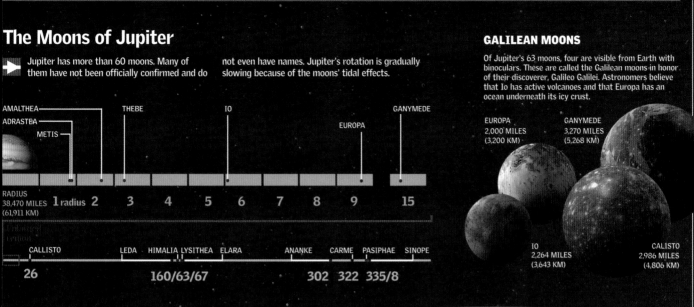

AMALTHEA
ADRASTEA
METIS
THEBE
IO
EUROPA
GANYMEDE

RADIUS
38,470 MILES
(61,911 KM)   1 radius   2   3   4   5   6   7   8   9   15

CALLISTO   LEDA HIMALIA LYSITHEA ELARA   ANANKE   CARME PASIPHAE SINOPE

26   160/63/67   302   322 335/8

GALILEAN MOONS

Of Jupiter's 63 moons, four are visible from Earth with binoculars. These are called the Galilean moons in honor of their discoverer, Galileo Galilei. Astronomers believe that Io has active volcanoes and that Europa has an ocean underneath its icy crust.

EUROPA
2,000 MILES
(3,200 KM)

GANYMEDE
3,270 MILES
(5,268 KM)

IO
2,264 MILES
(3,643 KM)

CALISTO
2,986 MILES
(4,806 KM)

Winds

The winds on Jupiter blow in contiguous bands and opposing directions. The bands' small differences in temperature and chemical composition give the planet its multicolored appearance. Jupiter's inclement environment, in which winds blow at more than 370 miles per hour (600 km/h), can cause large storms, such as the Great Red Spot in the southern hemisphere of the planet. The Great Red Spot, which is 16,155 miles (26,000 km) long, is believed to be composed mainly of ammonia gas and clouds of ice.

16,160
miles
(26,000 km)
GREAT RED SPOT

RINGS

Jupiter's rings are made of dust from the planet's four inner moons. These rings were first seen in 1979 by the space probe Voyager 1 and later by Voyager 2.

OUTER GOSSAMER RING
INNER GOSSAMER RING
MAIN RING
HALO

RING MATERIAL

JUPITER'S MAGNETISM

Jupiter's magnetic field is 20,000 times stronger than the Earth's. Astronomers believe the field is caused by the electrical currents that are created by the rapid rotation of metallic hydrogen. Jupiter is surrounded by a huge magnetic bubble, the magnetosphere. The magnetosphere's tail reaches more than 370,000,000 miles (600,000,000 km)—beyond the orbit of Saturn.

ATMOSPHERE

surrounds the inner liquid layers and the solid core. It is 620 miles thick (1,000 km).

89.8%
Hydrogen

10.2%
Helium
With traces of methane and ammonia

Jupiter's magnetosphere is the largest object in the solar system. It varies in size and shape in response to the solar wind, which is composed of the particles continuously radiated from the Sun.

400,000,000
miles
(650,000,000 km)

The Lord of the Rings

S aturn is the solar system's second largest planet. Like Jupiter, it is a large ball of gas surrounding a small, solid core. Saturn was the most distant planet discovered before the invention of the telescope. To the naked eye, it looks like a yellowish star, but with the help of a telescope, its rings are clearly visible. Ten times farther from the Sun than the Earth, Saturn is the least dense planet. If an ocean could be found large enough to hold it, Saturn would float.

Rings

Saturn's rings, the brightest rings in the solar system, are made of rock and ice and orbit Saturn's equator. The rings are probably remains of destroyed comets that were trapped by Saturn's gravitational field.

ENCKE DIVISION
A small gap that separates ring A into two parts

F RING
The farthest visible ring

A RING
Saturn's outer ring

CASSINI DIVISION
3,100 miles (5,000 km) wide, it is located between the A and B rings.

B RING
Saturn's brightest and widest ring

C RING
Saturn's only transparent ring

D RING
The closest ring to the surface of Saturn—so near that it almost touches the planet

RINGS G AND E

310 miles (500 km)

9,100 miles (14,600 km)

15,800 miles (25,500 km)

10,900 miles (17,500 km)

5,300 miles (8,500 km)

2,200 miles (3,500 km)

THICKNESS AND WIDTH
Although Saturn's rings are very wide, their thickness is sometimes less than 33 feet (10 m).

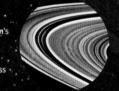

The Moons of Saturn

Saturn has more than 45 moons, making Saturn's family of moons one of the largest in the solar system. The sizes of the moons vary from Titan's 3,200 miles (5,150 km) to tiny Calypso's 10 miles (16 km).

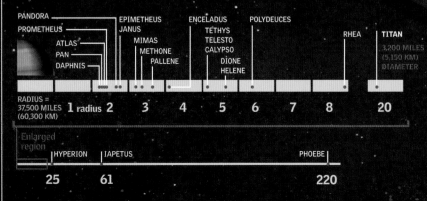

PANDORA
PROMETHEUS
EPIMETHEUS
JANUS
ATLAS
PAN
DAPHNIS
MIMAS
METHONE
PALLENE
ENCELADUS
TETHYS
TELESTO
CALYPSO
DIONE
HELENE
POLYDEUCES
RHEA
TITAN
3,200 MILES
(5,150 KM)
DIAMETER

RADIUS = 37,500 MILES (60,300 KM)

1 radius 2   3   4   5   6   7   8   20

Enlarged region

HYPERION   IAPETUS   PHOEBE

25   61   220

Titan has a larger diameter than Mercury. It has an atmosphere that is mostly made of nitrogen.

Surface

▶ Like Jupiter, Saturn has a surface of clouds that form bands because of the planet's rotation. Saturn's clouds are less turbulent and less colorful than Jupiter's. The higher, white clouds reach temperatures of -220° F (-140° C). A layer of haze extends above the clouds.

HAZE

WHITE CLOUDS

DEEP AND ORANGE CLOUDS

BLUISH CLOUDS

WINDS

Saturn's winds generally reach speeds of about 220 miles per hour (360 km/h), causing strong storms.

Gaseous Exterior

▶ Saturn and Jupiter differ very little in their composition. Both are gaseous balls surrounding solid cores. What sets Saturn apart are its rings, formed by clustered pieces of ice that range in size from small particles to large chunks. Each particle in a ring is a satellite orbiting Saturn. From the Earth, the massed debris seems to form large structures, but each discrete piece actually has its own orbit.

ATMOSPHERE

<1%
Sulfur gives it a yellowish appearance.

2%
Helium

97%
Hydrogen

COMPONENTS
The main components of Saturn's atmosphere are hydrogen (97%) and helium (2%). The rest is composed of sulfur, methane, and other gases.

CHARACTERISTICS

CONVENTIONAL PLANET SYMBOL   ♄

ESSENTIAL DATA

Average distance from the Sun	887,000,000 miles (1,427,000,000 km)
Solar orbit (Saturnine year)	29 years 154 days
Equatorial diameter	74,940 miles (120,600 km)
Orbital speed	6 miles per second (10 km/s)
Mass*	95
Gravity*	0.92
Density	0.4 ounce per cubic inch (0.7 g/cu cm)
Average temperature	-193° F (-125° C)
Atmosphere	Very dense
Moons	More than 45

*In both cases, Earth = 1

AXIS INCLINATION

26.7°
One rotation lasts 10 hours and 39 minutes.

15,500 miles (25,000 km)

9,300 miles (15,000 km)

9,300 miles (15,000 km)

OUTER MANTLE
This layer is formed by liquid molecular hydrogen.

ATMOSPHERE
Mainly hydrogen and helium

INNER MANTLE
It is made up of liquid metallic hydrogen.

CORE
Composed of rock and metallic elements, such as silicates and iron

21,600°F
(12,000° C)

Uranus Without Secrets

To the unaided eye, Uranus looks like a star at the limit of visibility. It is the seventh farthest planet from the Sun and the third largest planet in the solar system. One peculiarity distinguishing it from the other planets is its anomalous axis of rotation, tilted nearly 98 degrees around the plane of its orbit, so that one or the other of Uranus's poles points toward the Sun. Astronomers speculate that, during its formation, Uranus may have suffered an impact with a protoplanet, which could have altered Uranus's tilt. Uranus's orbit is so large that the planet takes 84 years to completely orbit the Sun. Uranus's period of rotation is 17 hours and 14 minutes.

MAGNETIC FIELD

Uranus generates a magnetic field 50 times more powerful than Earth's. This field is not centered on the planet, but is offset and tilted 60 degrees from Uranus's axis. If this were the case on Earth, the magnetic north pole would be located in Morocco. Unlike other planets, Uranus's magnetic field originates in the planet's mantle, not its core.

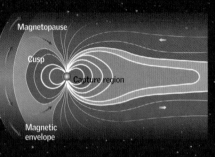

Magnetopause

Cusp

Capture region

Magnetic envelope

Some scientists suggest that Uranus's anomalous magnetic field may indicate that the convection of Uranus's core has stopped because of cooling—or, perhaps, that the planet is currently undergoing a magnetic inversion, as has happened on the Earth.

Composition

Uranus's core is made of abundant amounts of silicates and ice. The planet is almost four times larger than the Earth, and its atmosphere is made up of hydrogen, helium, and methane. Uranus has an almost horizontal tilt, causing it to have very long seasons.

CORE
Made up of silicates and ice

INNER MANTLE
Probably icy water, methane, and ammonia. (According to some models, the materials of the mantle and core do not form layers.)

OUTER MANTLE
Composed primarily of hydrogen and helium, as well as a small amount of methane

ATMOSPHERE
Uranus's atmosphere is made up of hydrogen, methane, helium, and small amounts of acetylene and other hydrocarbons.

6,200 MILES (10,000 KM)

10,600 MILES (17,000 KM)

6,200 MILES (10,000 KM)

CHARACTERISTICS

CONVENTIONAL PLANET SYMBOL ♅

ESSENTIAL DATA

Average distance from the Sun	1,780,000,000 miles (2,870,000,000 km)
Solar orbit (Uranian year)	84 years 4 days
Equatorial diameter	32,200 miles (51,800 km)
Orbital speed	4 miles per second (7 km/s)
Mass*	14.5
Gravity*	0.89
Density	0.8 ounce per cubic inch (1.3 g/cu cm)
Average temperature	-346° F (-210° C)
Atmosphere	Less dense
Moons	27

* In both cases, Earth = 1

AXIS INCLINATION

97.9°

One rotation lasts 17 hours and 14 minutes.

-346° F
(-210° C)
AVERAGE TEMPERATURE

85%
Hydrogen

3%
Methane

12%
Helium

EPSILON
LAMBDA
DELTA
GAMMA
ETA
BETA
ALPHA

4
5
6
1986U2R

Rings

Like all giant planets of the solar system, Uranus has a ring system, but it is much darker than Saturn's and more difficult to see. The planet's 11 rings, which orbit the planet's equator, were discovered in 1977. In 1986, they were explored by Voyager 2.

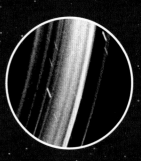

Satellites

Uranus has 27 moons. The first four were discovered in 1787, and another 10 were identified in 1986 by the space probe Voyager 2. Uranus's moons were named in honor of characters from the works of William Shakespeare and Alexander Pope, a naming convention that distinguishes them from the other moons in the solar system. Some of Uranus's moons are large, but most measure only dozens of miles.

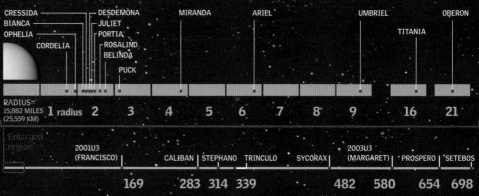

CRESSIDA
BIANCA
OPHELIA
CORDELIA
DESDEMONA
JULIET
PORTIA
ROSALIND
BELINDA
PUCK
MIRANDA
ARIEL
UMBRIEL
TITANIA
OBERON

RADIUS
15,882 MILES
(25,559 KM)

1 radius   2   3   4   5   6   7   8   9   16   21

Enlarged region

2001U3 (FRANCISCO)   CALIBAN   STEPHANO   TRINCULO   SYCORAX   2003U3 (MARGARET)   PROSPERO   SETEBOS

169   283   314   339   482   580   654   698

MOONS

Uranus has small, dark moons, discovered by Voyager 2, as well as bigger moons, such as Miranda, Ariel, Umbriel, Oberon, and Titania. These last two are approximately 930 miles (1,500 km) in diameter.

Miranda, only 293 miles (472 km) in diameter, is the smallest of Uranus's five main moons. It has an irregular surface with grooves and a bright mark.

TITANIA
980 MILES
(1,578 KM)

UMBRIEL
730 MILES
(1,170 KM)

MIRANDA
293 MILES
(472 KM)

OBERON
946 MILES
(1,522 KM)

ARIEL
720 MILES
(1,158 KM)

Surface

For a long time, Uranus was believed to have a smooth surface. The Hubble Space Telescope, however, showed that Uranus is a dynamic planet that has the solar system's brightest clouds and a fragile ring system that wobbles like an unbalanced wheel.

REFRACTION OF RAYS

1. In Uranus, sunlight is reflected by a curtain of clouds that lie underneath a layer of methane.

ATMOSPHERE   SUNLIGHT
URANUS

2. When sunlight passes through this layer, the methane absorbs the red light waves and lets the blue light waves pass through, producing the planet's hue.

ATMOSPHERE   SUNLIGHT
URANUS

Neptune: Deep Blue

Seen from our planet, Neptune appears as a faint, blue point invisible to the naked eye. Images sent to Earth by Voyager 2 show the planet as a remarkably blue sphere, an effect produced by the presence of methane in the outer part of Neptune's atmosphere. The farthest of the gaseous planets, Neptune is 30 times farther from the Sun than the Earth is. Its rings and impressive clouds are noteworthy, as is its resemblance to Uranus. Neptune is of special interest to astronomers because, before its discovery, its existence and location were predicted on the basis of mathematical calculations.

Moons

Neptune has 13 natural satellites, nine of which are named. Triton and Nereid were the first moons observed by telescope from Earth. The 11 remaining moons were observed from space by the U.S. space probe Voyager 2. All the names of Neptune's satellites correspond to ancient Greek marine deities.

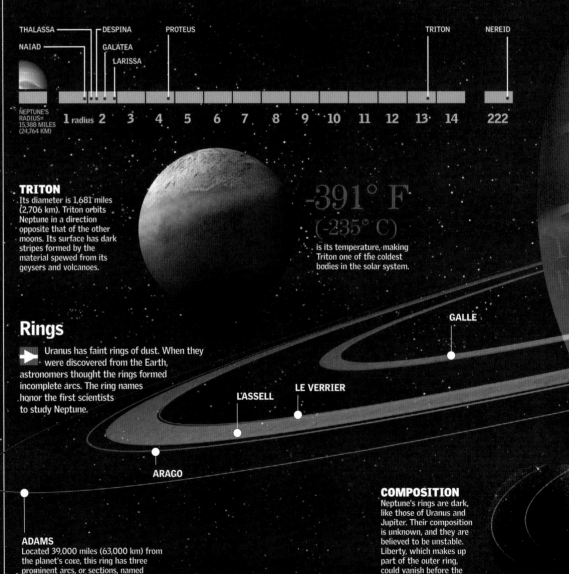

THALASSA — DESPINA — PROTEUS — TRITON — NEREID
NAIAD — GALATEA — LARISSA

NEPTUNE'S RADIUS= 15,388 MILES (24,764 KM)

1 radius 2 3 4 5 6 7 8 9 10 11 12 13 14 222

TRITON
Its diameter is 1,681 miles (2,706 km). Triton orbits Neptune in a direction opposite that of the other moons. Its surface has dark stripes formed by the material spewed from its geysers and volcanoes.

-391° F
(-235° C)
is its temperature, making Triton one of the coldest bodies in the solar system.

1,200 miles per hour 2,000 km/h

Rings

Uranus has faint rings of dust. When they were discovered from the Earth, astronomers thought the rings formed incomplete arcs. The ring names honor the first scientists to study Neptune.

GALLE

L'ASSELL   LE VERRIER

ARAGO

ADAMS
Located 39,000 miles (63,000 km) from the planet's core, this ring has three prominent arcs, or sections, named Liberty, Fraternity, and Equality.

COMPOSITION
Neptune's rings are dark, like those of Uranus and Jupiter. Their composition is unknown, and they are believed to be unstable. Liberty, which makes up part of the outer ring, could vanish before the 22nd century.

Surface

White methane clouds surround Neptune, circulating at some of the fastest speeds in the solar system. Neptune's winds reach 1,200 miles per hour (2,000 km/h) from east to west, swirling against the direction of the planet's rotation.

Ascending winds

Descending winds

THE GREAT SPOT
This giant storm, called the Great Dark Spot, was first seen on the surface of Neptune in 1989 and was as large as the Earth. By 1994, it had disappeared.

Hard Heart

According to some models, Neptune has a rocky silicate core, covered by a mantle of icy water, ammonia, hydrogen, and methane. According to some models, however, the materials of the mantle and core do not form layers.

CORE
Made up of silicates and ice

3,700 miles (6,000 km)

8,700 miles (14,000 km)

4,500 miles (7,200 km)

INNER MANTLE
Probably icy water, methane, and ammonia

OUTER MANTLE
Composed primarily of hydrogen and helium, as well as a small amount of methane

ATMOSPHERE
Banded, like the atmospheres of the other gas giants, Neptune's atmosphere forms a cloud system at least as active as Jupiter's.

Hydrogen

10.2%
Helium

CHARACTERISTICS

CONVENTIONAL PLANET SYMBOL ♆

ESSENTIAL DATA	
Average distance from the Sun	2,800,000,000 miles (4,500,000,000 km)
Solar orbit (Neptunian year)	164 years 264 days
Equatorial diameter	30,800 miles (49,500 km)
Orbital speed	3.4 miles per second (5.5 km/s)
Mass*	17.2
Gravity*	1.12
Density	1 ounce per cubic inch (1.6 g/cu cm)
Average temperature	-330° F (-200° C)
Atmosphere	Dense
Moons	13

*In both cases, Earth = 1.

AXIS INCLINATION
28.3°
One rotation lasts 16 hours and 36 minutes.

Pluto: Now a Dwarf

Pluto stopped being the ninth planet of the solar system in 2006 when the International Astronomical Union decided to change the classification of cold, distant Pluto to that of dwarf planet. This tiny body in our solar system has never had an imposing profile, and it has not yet been possible to study it closely. All that is known about Pluto comes through observations made from the Earth or Earth orbit, such as those made by the Hubble Space Telescope. Despite the lack of information gathered about Pluto, it is notable for its unique orbit, the tilt of its axis, and its location within the Kuiper belt. All these characteristics make Pluto especially intriguing.

A Double World

Pluto and its largest satellite, Charon, have a very special relationship. They have been called double planets—the diameter of Charon is about that of Pluto. One theory hypothesizes that Charon was formed from ice that was torn from Pluto when another object collided with the dwarf planet.

PLUTO

ROTATION AXIS

CHARON

Surface

Only a little is known about Pluto but the Hubble Space Telescope showed a surface covered by a frozen mixture of nitrogen and methane. The presence of solid methane indicates that its temperature is less than -333° F (-203° C), but the dwarf planet's temperature varies according to its place in orbit, ranging between 30 and 50 astronomical units from the Sun.

SYNCHRONIZED ORBITS

The orbital arrangement of Pluto and Charon is unique. Each always faces the other, making the two seem connected by an invisible bar. The synchronization of the two bodies is such that an observer on one side of Pluto would be able to see Charon, but another observer standing on the other side of the planet could not see this moon due to the curvature of the planet.

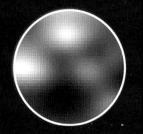

BEST VIEW OF PLUTO AVAILABLE

Moons

In addition to Charon, which was discovered in 1978, Pluto is orbited by two additional moons, Nix and Hydra, first observed in 2005. Unlike the surface of Pluto, which is made of frozen nitrogen, methane, and carbon dioxide, Charon appears to be covered with ice, methane, and carbon dioxide. One theory holds that the matter that formed this satellite was ejected from Pluto as a result of a collision, an origin similar to that ascribed to Earth's moon.

DENSITY

Charon's density is between 0.7 and 0.8 ounce per cubic inch (1.2 and 1.3 g/cu cm), indicating that its composition does not include much rock.

730 miles (1,172 km)

Charon's diameter—half of Pluto's

Composition

Scientific calculations have deduced that 75 percent of Pluto consists of a mixture of rocks and ice. This frozen surface is made up of 98 percent nitrogen, as well as traces of solidified carbon monoxide and methane. Recently scientists have concluded that

Pluto is an object that belongs to the Kuiper belt, a group of objects left over from the formation of the outer planets. In addition to large amounts of frozen nitrogen, Pluto has simple molecules containing hydrogen and oxygen, the building blocks of life.

ATMOSPHERE
Pluto's very thin atmosphere freezes and falls to the dwarf planet's surface as Pluto moves toward its aphelion.

Nitrogen

2%

Methane
With some traces of carbon monoxide

CRUST
The crust of this dwarf planet is made of methane and water frozen on the surface.

270 miles (434 km)

CORE
The core is made of iron, nickel, and silicates.

570 miles (920 km)

MANTLE
The mantle is a layer of frozen water.

NEW HORIZONS MISSION
The first space probe to be sent to Pluto was launched on January 19, 2006. It is to reach the dwarf planet in July 2015 and achieve the first flyby of Pluto and Charon.

CHARACTERISTICS

CONVENTIONAL PLANET SYMBOL ♇

ESSENTIAL DATA

Average distance from the Sun	3,700,000,000 miles (5,900,000,000 km)
Solar orbit (Plutonian year)	247.9 years
Equatorial diameter	1,400 miles (2,247 km)
Orbital speed 3 miles per second	(4.8 km/s)
Mass*	0.002
Gravity*	0.067
Density	1.2 ounces per cubic inch (2.05 g/cu cm)
Average temperature	-380° F (-230° C)
Atmosphere	Very thin
Moons	3

* In both cases, Earth = 1

AXIS INCLINATION

122°
One rotation lasts 6.387 Earth days.

A PECULIAR ORBIT
Pluto's orbit is noticeably elliptical, and it is tilted 17° from the plane of the planets' orbits. The distance between Pluto and the Sun varies from 2,500,000,000 to 4,300,000,000 miles (4,000,000,000 to 7,000,000,000 km). During each 248-year orbit, Pluto orbits closer to the Sun than Neptune for nearly 20 years. Although Pluto appears to cross paths with Neptune, it is impossible for them to collide.

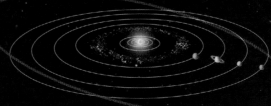

6,387
terrestrial days is the time Pluto takes to complete one rotation.

Distant Worlds

Farther even than Neptune, the eighth planet, we find frozen bodies smaller than the Earth's Moon—the more than 100,000 objects forming the Kuiper belt, the frozen boundary of our solar system. Recently astronomers of the International Astronomical Union decided to reclassify Pluto as a dwarf planet because of its size and eccentric orbit. Periodic comets (comets that appear at regular intervals) originate in the Kuiper belt. Nonperiodic comets, on the other hand, come from the Oort cloud, a gigantic sphere surrounding the entire solar system. ●

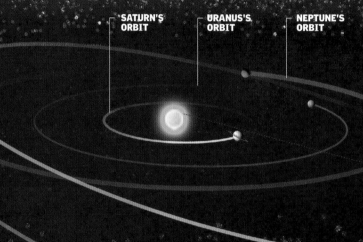

SATURN'S ORBIT

URANUS'S ORBIT

NEPTUNE'S ORBIT

PLUTO'S ORBIT

Kuiper Belt

➤ Extending outward from the orbit of Neptune are many frozen worlds similar in some ways to planets but much smaller. They are located in the Kuiper belt, the frozen boundary of our solar system. So far, almost a thousand objects have been cataloged, including Quaoar, which has a diameter of 810 miles (1,300 km). The Kuiper belt, estimated to contain more than 100,000 bodies of ice and rock larger than 60 miles (100 km) in diameter (including Pluto), spreads out in the shape of a wide ring. Many of the comets that approach the Sun come from the Kuiper belt.

1,410 miles (2,274 km)

is the diameter of Pluto—750 miles (1,200 km) smaller than the Earth's Moon. Because of its size and orbit, Pluto is considered a dwarf planet instead of a planet.

Comparable Sizes

The discovery of Quaoar in 2002 allowed scientists to find the link they had long looked for between the Kuiper belt and the origin of the solar system. Quaoar's almost circular orbit helped prove that some objects both belong to the Kuiper belt and orbit the Sun. At the official meeting of the International Astronomical Union, on August 24, 2006, Pluto was reclassified from a planet to a dwarf planet. For the time being, any further objects discovered in the Kuiper belt will be classified in the same category.

QUAOAR
has a diameter of 810 miles (1,300 km).

SEDNA
Its diameter is estimated at 1,000 miles (1,600 km).

PLUTO
possesses a diameter of 1,400 miles (2,300 km).

ERIS
Larger than Pluto, its diameter is about 1,900 miles (3,000 km).

200
OR MORE, POSSIBLE EXTRASOLAR PLANETS HAVE BEEN DETECTED.

ERIS

THE FARTHEST ONE

Eris is 97 astronomical units (9,040,000,000 miles [14,550,000,000 km]) from the Sun, making it the most distant object observed in the solar system. This dwarf planet follows an oval, eccentric orbit that takes 560 years to complete. The dwarf planet measures about 1,900 miles (3,000 km) in diameter, and traces of methane ice have been detected on its surface.

Construction Debris: Asteroids and Meteorites

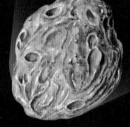

E ver since the formation of the solar system, the melting, collision, and rupture of various materials played an essential role in the formation of the planets. Remnants of this process remain in the form of rock debris, which serves as witnesses to the formation of the solar system. These objects are also associated with episodes that influenced subsequent evolutionary processes on Earth. They are a possible cause of the mass extinction of dinosaurs more than 60 million years ago. ●

Extraterrestrial

One of the main goals of scientist who study meteorites is to understand their nature. Meteoric material holds extraterrestrial solids and gases. Scientific tests have confirmed that some meteorites are from the Moon or Mars, but most meteorites are associated with asteroids. The samples obtained from meteorites are analyzed and classified by their composition.

A HUGE METEORITE STRIKES

A meteorite is an object from space that does not completely vaporize as it penetrates the Earth's atmosphere. Larger meteorites can form a crater when they strike the Earth. Shown is the impact of an exceptionally large meteorite, such as the one that many scientists believed might have led to the extinction of dinosaurs and many other species about 65 million years ago.

1. **EXPLOSION**
The friction created as a meteorite falls through the air increases its temperature. This is how an ignition process is started.

7 miles per second
(12 km/s) **IMPACT VELOCITY**

43 miles per second (70 km/s)

2. **DIVISION**
The fragmentation of a meteorite causes a visual effect called a shooting star.

3. **IMPACT**
The collision of the meteorite compresses and excavates the ground, leaving a crater.

TYPES OF METEORITES

STONY
meteorites contain silicate minerals. They are subdivided into chondrites and achondrites.

IRON
meteorites contain a high percentage of iron and nickel compounds. They are created in the rupture of asteroids.

MESOSIDERITES
contain similar quantities of iron, nickel, and silicates.

Asteroids

▶ Also called minor planets, they are the millions of rock and metal fragments of various shapes and sizes that orbit the Sun. They are mostly located in a belt between the orbits of Mars and Jupiter, but a few, such as those that belong to the Amor, Apollo, and Aten asteroid groups, orbit closer to Earth.

15%

The percentage of the total mass of the asteroids compared with the mass of the Moon

HIDALGO

completes a solar orbit every 14 Earth years.

ATEN

AMOR

APOLLO

MAIN ASTEROID BELT

The Trojans trace an orbit similar to Jupiter's, one group in front of the planet and another behind it.

Mars's Orbit

Jupiter's Orbit

Tighten Your Belt

▶ More than a million asteroids at least a mile in diameter are distributed in the main asteroid belt. Ceres was the first asteroid discovered (in 1801). It is the largest known asteroid, with a diameter of 580 miles (932 km).

KIRKWOOD

The Kirkwood gaps are the open areas in the main asteroid belt that are devoid of asteroids.

TYPES OF ASTEROIDS

Despite a great variety in size and shape, three types of minor planets, or asteroids, are known. Classified by their composition, they are grouped as siliceous, carbonaceous, and metallic.

IDA

An asteroid 35 miles (56 km) long, its surface is marked by collisions with other bodies.

Ferrous-type rocks dominate its composition.

Those with a Tail

Comets are small, deformed objects a few miles in diameter that are normally frozen and dark. Made of dust, rock, gases, and organic molecules rich in carbon, comets are usually found in orbits beyond that of Neptune in the Kuiper belt or in the Oort cloud. Occasionally a comet, such as Halley's comet, veers toward the interior of the solar system, where its ice is heated and sublimates, forming a head and long, spectacular tails of gases and dust.

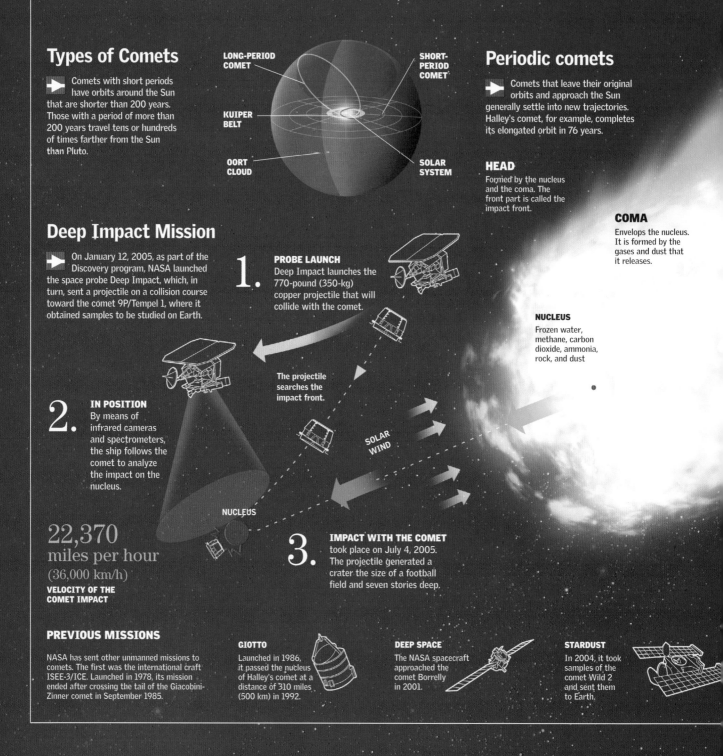

Types of Comets

Comets with short periods have orbits around the Sun that are shorter than 200 years. Those with a period of more than 200 years travel tens or hundreds of times farther from the Sun than Pluto.

LONG-PERIOD COMET

SHORT-PERIOD COMET

KUIPER BELT

OORT CLOUD

SOLAR SYSTEM

Periodic comets

Comets that leave their original orbits and approach the Sun generally settle into new trajectories. Halley's comet, for example, completes its elongated orbit in 76 years.

HEAD
Formed by the nucleus and the coma. The front part is called the impact front.

COMA
Envelops the nucleus. It is formed by the gases and dust that it releases.

Deep Impact Mission

On January 12, 2005, as part of the Discovery program, NASA launched the space probe Deep Impact, which, in turn, sent a projectile on a collision course toward the comet 9P/Tempel 1, where it obtained samples to be studied on Earth.

1. **PROBE LAUNCH**
Deep Impact launches the 770-pound (350-kg) copper projectile that will collide with the comet.

The projectile searches the impact front.

NUCLEUS
Frozen water, methane, carbon dioxide, ammonia, rock, and dust

2. **IN POSITION**
By means of infrared cameras and spectrometers, the ship follows the comet to analyze the impact on the nucleus.

SOLAR WIND

NUCLEUS

22,370
miles per hour
(36,000 km/h)
VELOCITY OF THE COMET IMPACT

3. **IMPACT WITH THE COMET**
took place on July 4, 2005. The projectile generated a crater the size of a football field and seven stories deep.

PREVIOUS MISSIONS

NASA has sent other unmanned missions to comets. The first was the international craft ISEE-3/ICE. Launched in 1978, its mission ended after crossing the tail of the Giacobini-Zinner comet in September 1985.

GIOTTO
Launched in 1986, it passed the nucleus of Halley's comet at a distance of 310 miles (500 km) in 1992.

DEEP SPACE
The NASA spacecraft approached the comet Borrelly in 2001.

STARDUST
In 2004, it took samples of the comet Wild 2 and sent them to Earth.

THE HEAD
The head of a comet can measure 62,000 miles (100,000 km) or more in diameter.

TAIL

HEAD

ION TAIL
The trail of suspended gases generates a low-intensity, luminous region with a bluish color. The gas molecules lose an electron and therefore have an electrical charge.

DUST TAIL
The suspended dust particles trail behind the comet, reflecting sunlight and making the luminous tail visible.

FORMATION OF THE TAIL AND HEAD

Because of the effects of solar radiation and the solar wind, gases and dust are released from an accelerating comet. The dust particles tend to form a curving trail, which is less sensitive to the pressure of the solar wind. As the comet leaves the confines of the solar system, its tails coincide once more, but they disappear as the nucleus cools down and ceases releasing gases.

Close to the Sun, the tails reach maximum length.

As the comet moves away from the Sun, its tails disappear.

Sun   Earth   Mars

Jupiter   Comet orbit

The Earth and the Moon

I n the beginning, the Earth was an incandescent mass that slowly began to cool, allowing the continents to emerge and acquire their current form. Although many drastic changes took place during these early eras, our blue planet has still not stopped changing. It must be recognized that life on Earth would be impossible without the presence of the

AERIAL VIEW OF THE EARTH
In this partial image of the Earth, we can see
Bora-Bora, an island that forms part of the
Leeward Islands, located in French Polynesia.

atmosphere—the colorless, odorless, invisible layer of gases that surrounds us, giving us air to breathe and protecting us from the Sun's harmful radiation. Although the atmosphere is approximately 435 miles (700 km) thick, it has no clear boundary and fades into space until it finally disappears. ●

The Blue Planet

The Earth is known as the blue planet because of the color of the oceans that cover two thirds of its surface. This planet, the third planet from the Sun, is the only one where the right conditions exist to sustain life, something that makes the Earth special. It has liquid water in abundance, a mild temperature, and an atmosphere that protects it from objects that fall from outer space. The atmosphere also filters solar radiation thanks to its ozone layer. Slightly flattened at its poles and wider at its equator, the Earth takes 24 hours to revolve once on its axis.

The Phenomenon of Life

Water, in liquid form, makes it possible for life to exist on the Earth, the only planet where temperatures vary from 32° F to 212° F (0° C to 100° C), allowing water to exist as a liquid. The Earth's average distance from the Sun, along with certain other factors, allowed life to develop 3.8 billion years ago.

70%

of the Earth's surface is water. From space, the planet looks blue.

-76° F
(-60° C)

ONLY ICE
Mars is so far from the Sun that all its water is frozen.

32° to 212° F
(0° to 100° C)

3 STATES
On the Earth, water is found in all three of its possible states.

Above 212° F
(100° C)

ONLY STEAM
On Mercury or Venus, which are very close to the Sun, water would evaporate.

1. **EVAPORATION**
Because of the Sun's energy, the water evaporates, entering the atmosphere from oceans and, to a lesser extent, from lakes, rivers, and other sources on the continents.

EARTH MOVEMENTS

The Earth moves, orbiting the Sun and rotating on its own axis.

SUN

93,500,000 miles
(149,503,000 km)

ROTATION: The Earth revolves on its axis in 23 hours and 56 minutes.

REVOLUTION: It takes the Earth 365 days, 5 hours, and 57 minutes to travel once around the Sun.

The Moon, our only natural satellite, is four times smaller than the Earth and takes 27.32 days to orbit the Earth.

SOUTH POLE

AXIS
INCLINATION

ROTATION
AXIS

NORTH
POLE

23.5°

This is the inclination of the Earth's axis from the vertical. As the Earth orbits the Sun, different regions gradually receive more or less sunlight, causing the four seasons.

CHARACTERISTICS

CONVENTIONAL
PLANET
SYMBOL

ESSENTIAL DATA

Average distance to the Sun	93 million miles (150 million km)
Revolution around the Sun (Earth year)	365.25 days
Diameter at the equator	7,930 miles (12,756 km)
Orbiting speed	17 miles per second (27.79 km/s.)
Mass*	1
Gravity*	1

Density	3.2 ounces per cubic inch (5.52 g/cu cm)
Average temperature	59° F (15° C)

*In both cases, Earth = 1

AXIS INCLINATION

23.5°

One rotation lasts 23.56 hours.

3. PRECIPITATION

The atmosphere loses water through condensation. Gravity causes rain, snow, and hail. Dew and frost directly alter the state of the surface they cover.

Magnetism and Gravity

The Earth's magnetic field originates in the planet's outer core, where turbulent currents of molten iron generate both electric and magnetic fields. The orientation of the Earth's magnetism varies over time, causing the magnetic poles to fluctuate.

The Earth's core works as a magnet.

Magnetic force

Solid core

Mantle

The Earth's magnetic field is created by convective currents in its outer core.

The liquid outer core is in constant motion.

2. CONDENSATION

The Earth's winds transport moisture-laden air until weather conditions cause the water vapor to condense into clouds and eventually fall to the ground as rain or other forms of precipitation.

WHAT IT DOES

Some particles are attracted to the poles.

Van Allen belt

The magnetic field protects the Earth from the radiation of the solar wind.

Solar wind

Magnetic field lines

Magnetosphere

The Van Allen belts trap the particles from the solar wind, causing phenomena like the auroras.

Axis

Earth

Magnetic field tail

GRAVITY AND WEIGHT

Weight is the force of the gravity that acts on a body.

24 pounds (11 kg)

ON THE MOON

The Moon has less mass than the Earth and, as a result, less gravity.

154 pounds (70 kg)

ON EARTH

The object is drawn toward the Earth's center.

390 pounds (177 kg)

ON JUPITER

Jupiter has 300 times more mass than the Earth and therefore more gravity.

Journey to the Center of the Earth

W e live on the Earth, but do we know what we are standing on? The planet is made up of layers of various materials, such as solid and molten rock, which in turn are composed of such elements as iron, nickel, and silicon. Our atmosphere is the layer of gases surrounding our planet. One of these gases, oxygen, does a very special job—it permits life to exist. ●

Internal Structure

We live on a rocky surface similar to a shell. The rocks we live with are made mostly of oxygen and silicon, but underneath them is the mantle, made of much heavier rocks. The mantle also surrounds the inner and outer cores with a region of constantly boiling liquid metals, creating the convective currents that generate the Earth's magnetic field. The inner core, solid because of the great pressure put upon it, is the densest part of the planet.

HOW FAR HUMANS HAVE GONE

Mount Everest
5.5 miles
(8.85 km)

Continental penetration

Oceanic penetration

1 mile (1.7 km)

7.5 miles (12 km)

435 miles (700 km)

1,800 miles (2,900 km)

1,410 miles (2,270 km)

755 miles (1,216 km)

INNER CORE
is made of the same metals as the outer core, but, despite its high temperature, its center is solid because of the enormous pressure that compresses it.

OUTER CORE
The outer layer of the core is liquid, consisting of molten iron and nickel. Its temperature is lower than that of the inner core and it is under less pressure. The motion of the molten material produces the geomagnetic field.

INNER MANTLE
The solid, intermediate layer between the core and the crust. High-temperature S and P waves pass through it because of its contact with the core.

OUTER MANTLE
As a result of the high temperatures, the materials dilate and produce a continuous ascending movement that generates convection currents and the forces that cause the changes to the Earth's crust.

620 MILES (1,000 KM)

3,965 MILES (6,380 KM)

3,965 miles (6,380 km)

from the Earth's surface to its center.

EXOSPHERE

THERMOSPHERE

MESOSPHERE

STRATOSPHERE

TROPOSPHERE

Hydrosphere and Lithosphere

The lithosphere includes the crust and the upper portion of the mantle, and the hydrosphere includes liquid water, covering 71 percent of the Earth's surface in lakes, rivers, and five oceans.

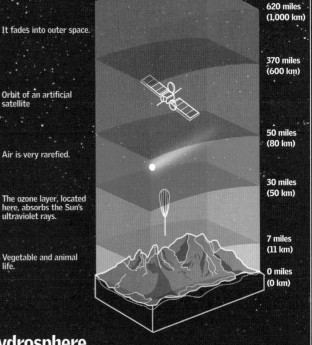

WITH ATMOSPHERE
The sunlight filters into the atmosphere. Winds distribute the heat, cooling the tropics and warming the poles.

WITHOUT ATMOSPHERE
Direct solar radiation. Differences in temperature between the equator and the poles would be far more pronounced.

Above the Surface

The existence of life on our planet would be impossible without the atmosphere that provides the air we breathe and the water we drink; it also protects us from the Sun's harmful radiation, while simultaneously maintaining mild temperatures by retaining the Sun's warmth. The atmosphere is about 435 miles thick (700 km) but lacks defined limits.

620 miles (1,000 km)

It fades into outer space.

370 miles (600 km)

Orbit of an artificial satellite

50 miles (80 km)

Air is very rarefied.

30 miles (50 km)

The ozone layer, located here, absorbs the Sun's ultraviolet rays.

7 miles (11 km)

Vegetable and animal life.

0 miles (0 km)

Lithosphere and Hydrosphere

The hydrosphere, the liquid part of the Earth, includes the oceans, lakes, rivers, underground waters, snow, and ice. It almost completely covers the crust, surrounds the shores of the continents, and covers 71 percent of the Earth's surface. The lithosphere is a superficial, elastic region that is 4 to 7 miles (6 to 11 km) thick under the oceans and up to 43 miles (70 km) thick under mountain ranges.

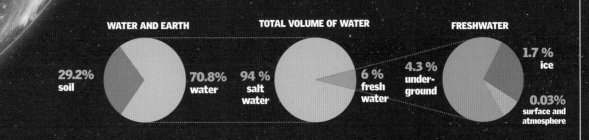

WATER AND EARTH

29.2% soil

70.8% water

TOTAL VOLUME OF WATER

94 % salt water

6 % fresh water

4.3 % underground

FRESHWATER

1.7 % ice

0.03% surface and atmosphere

Once Upon a Time

The Earth probably formed from material in the solar nebula—the cloud of gas and dust that led to the formation of the Sun. This material gradually grew into a larger and larger body that became a red-hot ball of rock and metal. Later the rocky crust formed, its surface cooling enough to allow the continents to appear. Even later the oceans arrived, as well as the tiny organisms that released oxygen into the atmosphere. Although much of this gas was initially consumed in chemical reactions, over time, it allowed the development of multicellular organisms and an explosion of life that took place at the start of the Paleozoic Era, 542 million years ago. ●

Continental Drift

We live on the continents, which are part of movable plates that drift across the Earth's surface at the rate a fingernail grows. 250 million years ago, India, Africa, Australia, and Antarctica were part of the same continent. When tectonic plates rub against each other, land and oceanic crust earthquakes occur. Where the plates separate, a rift forms. The mid-ocean ridges that run beneath the oceans are formed by lava that emerges from the rifts between tectonic plates. Where plates collide, a process called subduction takes place, in which the rocks of the oceanic floor are drawn under the continent and melt, reemerging in the form of volcanoes.

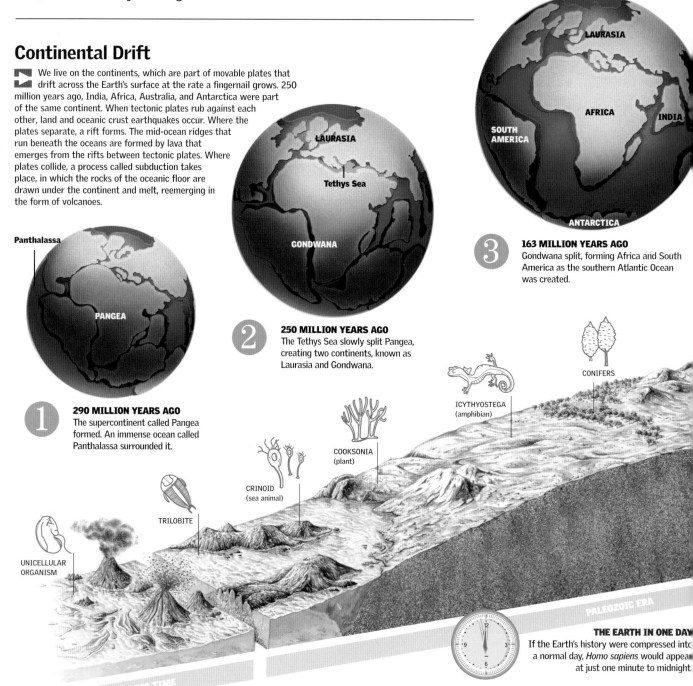

LAURASIA

Tethys Sea

GONDWANA

LAURASIA

AFRICA

INDIA

SOUTH AMERICA

ANTARCTICA

3 **163 MILLION YEARS AGO**
Gondwana split, forming Africa and South America as the southern Atlantic Ocean was created.

Panthalassa

PANGEA

2 **250 MILLION YEARS AGO**
The Tethys Sea slowly split Pangea, creating two continents, known as Laurasia and Gondwana.

1 **290 MILLION YEARS AGO**
The supercontinent called Pangea formed. An immense ocean called Panthalassa surrounded it.

CONIFERS

ICYTHYOSTEGA (amphibian)

COOKSONIA (plant)

CRINOID (sea animal)

TRILOBITE

UNICELLULAR ORGANISM

THE EARTH IN ONE DAY
If the Earth's history were compressed into a normal day, *Homo sapiens* would appear at just one minute to midnight

PALEOZOIC ERA

PRECAMBRIC TIME

Origin of the Earth

The Earth was formed 4.6 billion years ago from a cloud of dust and gas. In the beginning, it was a molten, constantly active, mass. As time passed, the Earth began to cool, and the atmosphere began to clear as rain fell, creating the oceans.

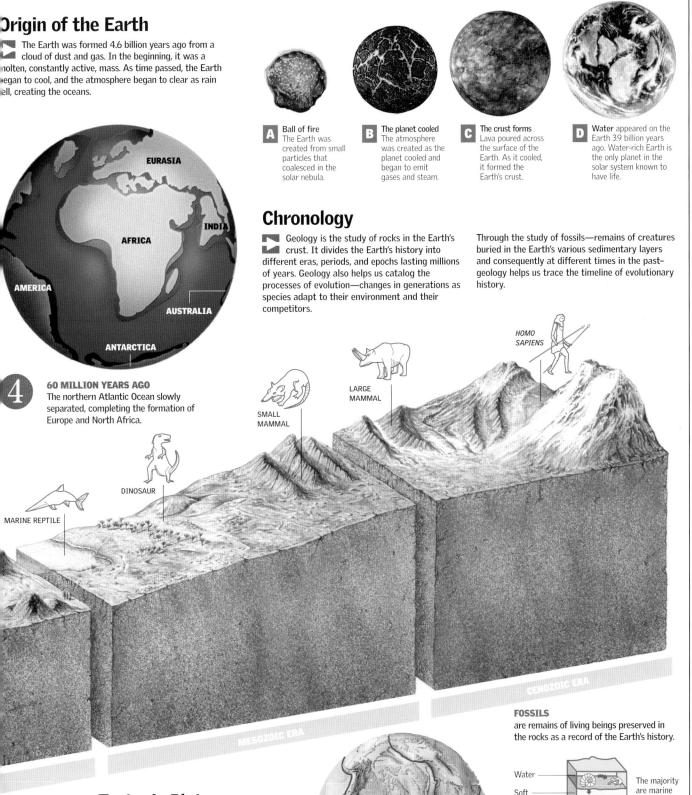

A Ball of fire
The Earth was created from small particles that coalesced in the solar nebula.

B The planet cooled
The atmosphere was created as the planet cooled and began to emit gases and steam.

C The crust forms
Lava poured across the surface of the Earth. As it cooled, it formed the Earth's crust.

D Water appeared on the Earth 3.9 billion years ago. Water-rich Earth is the only planet in the solar system known to have life.

EURASIA
INDIA
AFRICA
AMERICA
AUSTRALIA
ANTARCTICA

Chronology

Geology is the study of rocks in the Earth's crust. It divides the Earth's history into different eras, periods, and epochs lasting millions of years. Geology also helps us catalog the processes of evolution—changes in generations as species adapt to their environment and their competitors.

Through the study of fossils—remains of creatures buried in the Earth's various sedimentary layers and consequently at different times in the past—geology helps us trace the timeline of evolutionary history.

4 60 MILLION YEARS AGO
The northern Atlantic Ocean slowly separated, completing the formation of Europe and North Africa.

HOMO SAPIENS
LARGE MAMMAL
SMALL MAMMAL
DINOSAUR
MARINE REPTILE
MESOZOIC ERA
CENOZOIC ERA

Tectonic Plates

The surface of the Earth is shaped by tectonic plates. There are eight major plates, some of which even encompass entire continents. The plates' borders are marked by ocean trenches, cliffs, chains of volcanoes, and earthquake zones.

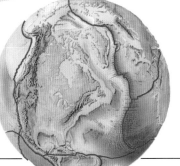

FOSSILS
are remains of living beings preserved in the rocks as a record of the Earth's history.

Water
Soft sediment
Hard sediment
Metamorphic rocks

The majority are marine shells.

At a certain depth, the pressure destroys the fossils.

Movements and Coordinates

Yes, it moves. The Earth rotates on its axis while simultaneously orbiting the Sun. The natural phenomena of night and day, seasons, and years are caused by these movements. To track the passage of time, calendars, clocks, and time zones were invented. Time zones are divided by meridians and assigned a reference hour according to their location. When traveling east, an hour is added with each time zone. An hour is subtracted during west-bound travel. ●

The Earth's Movements

Night and day, summer and winter, new year and old year result from the Earth's various movements during its orbit of the Sun. The most important motions are the Earth's daily rotation from west to east on its own axis and its revolution around the Sun. (The Earth follows an elliptical orbit that has the Sun at one of the foci of the ellipse, so the distance to the Sun varies slightly over the course of a year.)

ROTATION
1 DAY
The Earth revolves once on its axis in 23 hours and 56 minutes. We see this as day and night.

23°

REVOLUTION
1 YEAR
The Earth's orbit around the Sun lasts 365 days, 5 hours, and 57 minutes.

NUTATION
18.6 YEARS
is a sort of nod made by the Earth, causing the displacement of the geographic poles by nine arc seconds.

3°

PRECESSION
25,800 YEARS
A slow turning of the direction of the Earth's axis (similar to that of a top), caused by the Earth's nonspherical shape and the gravitational forces of the Sun and the Moon

47°

Equinox and Solstice

Every year, around June 21, the Northern Hemisphere reaches its maximum inclination toward the Sun (a phenomenon referred to as the summer solstice in the Northern Hemisphere and the winter solstice in the Southern Hemisphere). The North Pole receives sunlight all day, while the South Pole is covered in darkness. Between one solstice and another the equinoxes appear, which is when the axis of the Earth points toward the Sun and the periods of daylight and darkness are the same all over our planet.

June 20 or 21

Summer solstice in the Northern Hemisphere and winter solstice in the Southern Hemisphere. Solstices exist because of the tilt of the Earth's axis. The length of the day and the height of the Sun in the sky are greatest in summer and least in winter.

MEASUREMENT OF TIME
Months and days are charted by calendars and clocks, but the measurement of these units of time is neither a cultural nor an arbitrary construct. Instead, it is derived from the natural movements of the Earth.

March 20 or 21

Spring equinox in the Northern Hemisphere and autumn equinox in the Southern Hemisphere.
The Sun passes directly above the equator, and day and night have the same length.

SUN

September 21 or 22

Autumn equinox in the Northern Hemisphere and spring equinox in the Southern Hemisphere.
The Sun passes directly above the equator, and day and night have the same length.

PERIHELION
The point where the orbiting Earth most closely approaches the Sun (91 million miles [147 million km])

23.5°
TILT OF THE EARTH'S AXIS

93
**MILLION MILES
(149 MILLION KM)**

December 21 or 22

Winter solstice in the Northern Hemisphere and summer solstice in the Southern Hemisphere.
Solstices exist because of the tilt of the Earth's axis. The length of the day and the height of the Sun in the sky are greatest in summer and least in winter.

APHELION
The point in the Earth's orbit where it is farthest from the Sun (94 million miles [152 million km]). This occurs at the beginning of July.

Geographic Coordinates

Thanks to the grid formed by the lines of latitude and longitude, the position of any object on the Earth's surface can be easily located by using the intersection of the Earth's equator and the Greenwich meridian (longitude 0°) as a reference point. This intersection marks the midpoint between the Earth's poles.

THE EARTH'S ORBIT
About 365 days

1 day — THE DAYS
Period of time it takes the Earth to rotate on its axis

About 30 days — THE MONTHS
Each period of time, between 28 and 31 days, into which a year is divided

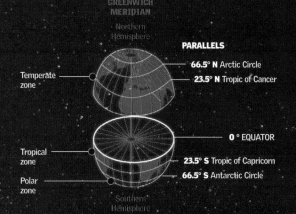

0°
GREENWICH MERIDIAN

Northern Hemisphere

PARALLELS

Temperate zone

66.5° N Arctic Circle
23.5° N Tropic of Cancer

Tropical zone

0 ° EQUATOR

23.5° S Tropic of Capricorn
66.5° S Antarctic Circle

Polar zone

Southern Hemisphere

Time Zones

The Earth is divided into 24 areas, or time zones, each one of which corresponds to an hour assigned according to the Coordinated Universal Time (UTC), using the Greenwich, England, meridian as the base meridian. One hour is added when crossing the meridian in an easterly direction, and one hour is subtracted when traveling west.

JET LAG

The human body's biological clock responds to the rhythms of light and dark based on the passage of night and day. Long air flights east or west interrupt and disorient the body's clock, causing a disorder known as jet lag. It can cause fatigue, irritability, nausea, headaches, and difficulty sleeping at night.

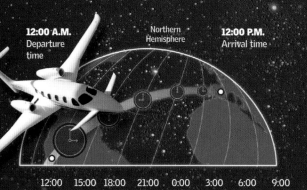

12:00 A.M.
Departure time

Northern Hemisphere

12:00 P.M.
Arrival time

12:00 15:00 18:00 21:00 0:00 3:00 6:00 9:00

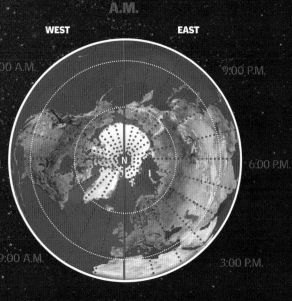

12:00 A.M.

WEST — EAST

3:00 A.M. — 9:00 P.M.

6:00 A.M. — 6:00 P.M.

N

9:00 A.M. — 3:00 P.M.

12:00 P.M.

The Moon and Tides

Romance and terror, mystery and superstition–all these emotions are responses to the Moon, the Earth's one natural satellite, which always hides one of its two faces. However, whatever symbolic meanings are attributed to the Moon, its gravitational pull has a concrete effect on the Earth—it is a cause of the tides. Depending on the distance of the Moon from the Earth, the gravitational pull exerted by the Moon varies in strength and so can high tides and low tides. To reach full height, tides need large open areas of ocean. For this reason, tides in closed or small bodies of water are much lower. ●

ORIGIN OF THE MOON
The most widely accepted theory of the Moon's origin suggests that an object the size of Mars collided with the Earth during its formation.

The ejected material scattered into space around the Earth, and over time, it coalesced into the Moon.

Aristarchus
Brightest spot on the Moon

Oceanus Procellarum
The largest sea, it is not well preserved.

VISIBLE FACE
Spotted with dark areas, it always faces the Earth.

Grimaldi

Gassendi

THE MOON'S MOVEMENTS

As the Moon orbits the Earth, it revolves on its own axis in such a way that it always shows the Earth the same side.

LUNAR MONTH
It takes 29.53 days to complete its phases.

SIDEREAL MONTH
It takes 27.32 days to orbit the Earth.

Visible face Moon

Hidden face

Earth

Lunar orbit

HIDDEN FACE
Invisible from the Earth, this side of the Moon was a mystery until 1959, when the Russian probe Luna 3 managed to photograph the hidden zone. Because of the greater thickness of the Moon's crust on this side, it has fewer seas.

The Tides

The water on the side of the Earth closest to the Moon feels the Moon's gravitational pull most intensely, and vice versa. Two tides are formed, and they track the Moon in its orbit around the Earth. However, they precede the Moon instead of being directly in line with it.

1 NEW MOON
SPRING TIDE
When the Sun and the Moon are aligned, the highest high tides and lowest low tides are produced.

2 FIRST QUARTER
NEAP TIDE
The Moon and the Sun are at right angles to the Earth, producing the lowest high tides and the highest low tides.

3 FULL MOON
SPRING TIDE
The Sun and the Moon align once again, and the Sun augments the Moon's gravitational pull, causing a second spring tide.

4 THIRD QUARTER
NEAP TIDE
The Moon and the Sun again form a right angle, causing a second neap tide.

KEY

Gravitational pull of the Moon

Gravitational pull of the Sun

● Influence on the tide by the gravitational pull of the Sun

● Influence on the tide by the gravitational pull of the Moon

Lunar orbit

Moon

Earth orbit

Sun

The Sun's gravity also influences the tides.

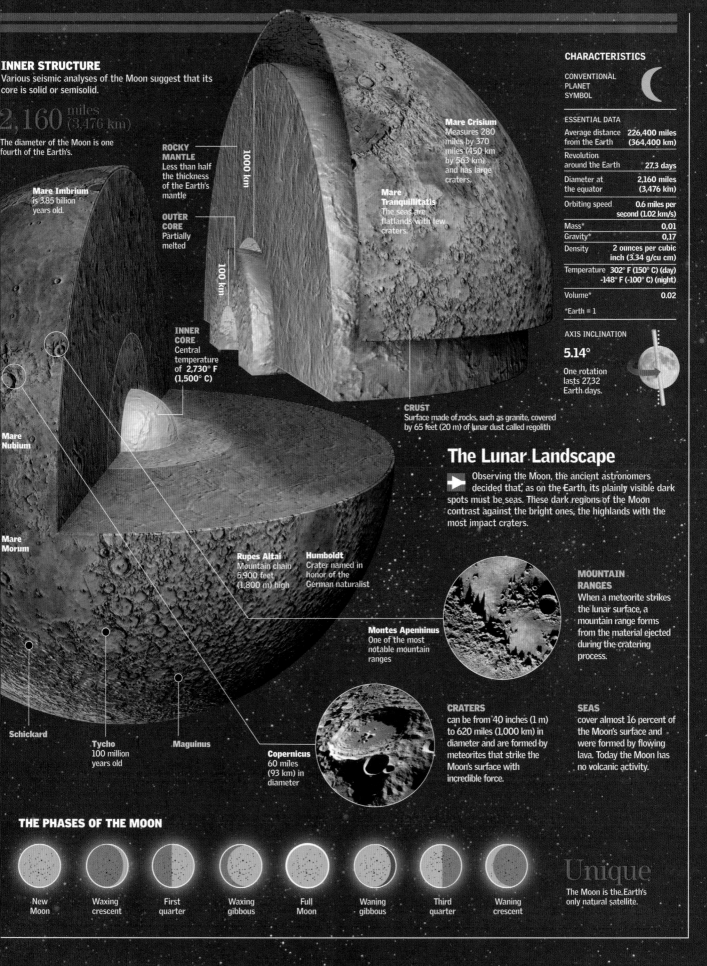

INNER STRUCTURE
Various seismic analyses of the Moon suggest that its core is solid or semisolid.

2,160 miles (3,476 km)
The diameter of the Moon is one fourth of the Earth's.

Mare Imbrium is 3.85 billion years old.

ROCKY MANTLE Less than half the thickness of the Earth's mantle

1000 km

OUTER CORE Partially melted

100 km

INNER CORE Central temperature of 2,730° F (1,500° C)

Mare Crisium Measures 280 miles by 370 miles (450 km by 563 km) and has large craters.

Mare Tranquillitatis The seas are flatlands with few craters.

Mare Nubium

Mare Morum

Rupes Altai Mountain chain 5,900 feet (1,800 m) high

Humboldt Crater named in honor of the German naturalist

Montes Apenninus One of the most notable mountain ranges

Schickard

Tycho 100 million years old

Maguinus

Copernicus 60 miles (93 km) in diameter

CRUST Surface made of rocks, such as granite, covered by 65 feet (20 m) of lunar dust called regolith

CHARACTERISTICS

CONVENTIONAL PLANET SYMBOL

ESSENTIAL DATA

Average distance from the Earth	226,400 miles (364,400 km)
Revolution around the Earth	27.3 days
Diameter at the equator	2,160 miles (3,476 km)
Orbiting speed	0.6 miles per second (1.02 km/s)
Mass*	0,01
Gravity*	0,17
Density	2 ounces per cubic inch (3.34 g/cu cm)
Temperature	302° F (150° C) (day) -148° F (-100° C) (night)
Volume*	0.02

*Earth = 1

AXIS INCLINATION
5.14°
One rotation lasts 27,32 Earth days.

The Lunar Landscape
Observing the Moon, the ancient astronomers decided that, as on the Earth, its plainly visible dark spots must be seas. These dark regions of the Moon contrast against the bright ones, the highlands with the most impact craters.

MOUNTAIN RANGES When a meteorite strikes the lunar surface, a mountain range forms from the material ejected during the cratering process.

CRATERS can be from 40 inches (1 m) to 620 miles (1,000 km) in diameter and are formed by meteorites that strike the Moon's surface with incredible force.

SEAS cover almost 16 percent of the Moon's surface and were formed by flowing lava. Today the Moon has no volcanic activity.

THE PHASES OF THE MOON

New Moon	Waxing crescent	First quarter	Waxing gibbous	Full Moon	Waning gibbous	Third quarter	Waning crescent

Unique
The Moon is the Earth's only natural satellite.

Eclipses

Typically four times a year, during the full or new moon, the centers of the Moon, the Sun, and the Earth become aligned, causing one of the most marvelous celestial phenomena: an eclipse. At these times, the Moon either passes in front of the Sun or passes through the Earth's shadow. The Sun—even during an eclipse—is not safe to look at directly, since it can cause irreparable damage to the eyes, such as burns on the retina. Special high-quality filters or indirect viewing by projecting the Sun's image on a sheet of paper are some of the ways in which this celestial wonder can be watched. Solar eclipses provide, in addition, a good opportunity for astronomers to conduct scientific research.

TOTAL LUNAR ECLIPSE, SEEN FROM THE EARTH

The orange color comes from sunlight that has been refracted and colored by the Earth's atmosphere

ANNUAL ECLIPSE OF THE SUN, SEEN FROM THE EARTH

Solar Eclipse

Solar eclipses occur when the Moon passes directly between the Sun and the Earth, casting a shadow along a path on the Earth's surface. The central cone of the shadow is called the umbra, and the area of partial shadow around it is called the penumbra. Viewers in the regions where the umbra falls on the Earth's surface see the Moon's disk completely obscure the Sun—a total solar eclipse. Those watching from the surrounding areas that are located in the penumbra see the Moon's disk cover only part of the Sun—a partial solar eclipse.

ALIGNMENT

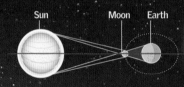

Sun   Moon   Earth

During a solar eclipse, astronomers take advantage of the blocked view of the Sun in order to use devices designed to study the Sun's atmosphere.

TYPES OF ECLIPSES

TOTAL
The Moon is between the Sun and the Earth and creates a cone-shaped shadow.

ANNULAR
The Sun appears larger than the Moon, and it remains visible around it.

PARTIAL
The Moon does not cover the Sun completely, so the Sun appears as a crescent.

SUNLIGHT

SUN'S APPARENT SIZE

400 times larger than the Moon

DISTANCE FROM THE SUN TO THE EARTH

400 times greater than the distance Earth to the Moon

Lunar Eclipse

When the Earth passes directly between the full Moon and the Sun, a lunar eclipse (which could be total, partial, or penumbral) occurs. Without the Earth's atmosphere, during each lunar eclipse, the Moon would become completely invisible (something that never happens). The totally eclipsed Moon's characteristic reddish color is caused by light refracted by the Earth's atmosphere. During a partial eclipse, on the other hand, part of the Moon falls in the shadow cone, while the rest is in the penumbra, the outermost, palest part. It is not dangerous to look at a lunar eclipse directly.

ALIGNMENT

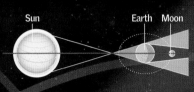

Sun · Earth · Moon

During an eclipse, the Moon is not completely black but appears reddish.

TYPES OF ECLIPSES

TOTAL
The Moon is completely in the shadow cone.

PARTIAL
The Moon is only partially inside the shadow cone.

PENUMBRAL
The Moon is in the penumbral cone.

Lunar orbit

Shadow cone

FULL MOON
TOTAL ECLIPSE

PARTIAL ECLIPSE

PENUMBRAL ECLIPSE

Shadow cone

NEW MOON
TOTAL ECLIPSE

EARTH

Penumbra cone

Earth orbit

THE ECLIPSE CYCLE

Eclipses repeat every 223 lunations—18 years and 11 days. These are called Saros periods.

ECLIPSES IN A YEAR

2	7	4
Minimum	Maximum	Average

ECLIPSES IN A SAROS

41	29	70
of the Sun	of the Moon	Total

OBSERVATION FROM EARTH

A black, polymer filter, with an optical density of 5.0, produces a clear orange image of the Sun.

Prevents retinal burns

SOLAR ECLIPSES
are different for each local observer.

LUNAR ECLIPSES
are the same for all observers.

MAXIMUM DURATION
8 minutes

MAXIMUM DURATION
100 minutes

ECLIPSES IN 2006 AND BEYOND

OF THE SUN	3/29 Total	9/22 Total	3/19 Partial	9/11 Partial	2/07 Total		1/26 Total		7/22 Total	1/15 Total	7/11 Total		1/4 Partial	11/25 Partial	5/20 Annular	11/13 Annular	5/10 Annular	11/3 Hybrid	4/29 Annular	10/23 Partial	3/20 Total	9/13 Partial
	2006		**2007**		**2008**		**2009**		**2010**		**2011**		**2012**		**2013**		**2014**		**2015**		**2016**
OF THE MOON	3/14 Partial	9/07 Partial	3/03 Total	8/28 Total	2/21 Total	8/16 Partial	2/9 Partial	7/7 Partial	6/26 Partial	12/21 Total	6/15 Total	12/10 Total	6/4 Partial	12/28 Partial	4/25 Partial	10/18 Partial	4/15 Total	10/08 Total	4/4 Total	9/28 Total

Observing the Universe

stronomy was born out of
humankind's need to measure
time and seasons, marking the
best times to plant. In ancient
times, the study of the stars
was mixed with superstition and ritual.
The megalithic monument Stonehenge,
found in southern England, is an example
of this. Today, thanks to advances in new
technologies, such as the giant telescopes

STONEHENGE
Located in Wiltshire (England), it was built in several phases over some 600 years—between 2200 and 1600 BC. The placement of most of its large stones has a relationship to the Moon and the Sun.

installed in various locations around the planet, we have discovered many new things about the universe. The VLT (Very Large Telescope), astronomy's new monster telescope located in Chile, is part of an attempt to find planets beyond the solar system, because many astronomers suspect that life is not exclusive to the Earth. ●

Astronomical Theories

For a long time, it was believed that the Earth was stationary. The Sun, the Moon, and the planets were thought to orbit it. To study the sky and calculate its movements, people began to build instruments, such as the astrolabe, armillary sphere, and telescope. The telescope revolutionized the conception of the universe. Instead of the Earth being at the center of the universe, it was suggested that the Earth and other planets travel around the Sun. The Roman Catholic Church opposed the idea and, for a time, persecuted dissident astronomers and banned their theories. ●

Geocentric Model

Before telescopes, binoculars, and modern observatories existed, little was known about the Earth. Many believed that the Earth was fixed and that the Sun, the Moon, and the five known planets orbited it in circles. This geocentric model was promoted by the Egyptian astronomer Claudius Ptolemy, who in the 2nd century AD compiled the astronomical ideas of the ancient Greek astronomers (in particular, those of Aristotle, who had proposed the Earth as the center of the universe, with the celestial objects revolving around it). Although other ancient astronomers, such as Aristarchus of Samus, proposed that the Earth was round and rotated around the Sun, Aristotle's ideas were accepted as true for 16 centuries, and at times Aristotle's ideas were defended and preserved by the Roman Catholic Church.

MEASUREMENTS

Noticing that the Sun, the Moon, and the stars moved in cycles, ancient civilizations found they could use the sky as both a clock and a calendar. However, ancient astronomers had difficulties performing the complex calculations needed to predict the positions of stars accurately enough to create a truly precise calendar. A useful tool developed to perform this task was the astrolabe. Its engraved plates reproduce the celestial sphere in two dimensions, allowing the elevations of the celestial bodies to be measured.

TIME
This astrolabe was used by ancient Persians. To them, astronomy functioned as a kind of agricultural calendar.

COSMIC CHARACTERS

2nd Century
Claudius Ptolemy
100-170

Resurrected and compiled the works of great Greek astronomers into two books. His postulates held undisputed authority for centuries.

16th Century
Nicolaus Copernicus
1473-1543

In his *De revolutionibus orbium coelestium*, the Polish astronomer postulated that the Sun—not the Earth—was the center of the universe. This concept is the foundation of our own astronomy..

17th Century
Johannes Kepler
1571-1630

The German astronomer, believer in Copernicus's heliocentric model, formulated three famous laws of planetary movement, which encouraged Galileo to publish his research.

Heliocentric Model

In 1543, a few months before his death, Nicolaus Copernicus published the book *De revolutionibus orbium coelestium*, inaugurating what is now known as the Copernican Revolution. The Polish astronomer developed the heliocentric theory (from *helios*, the Greek word for "the Sun"), which contradicted the geocentric theory. Copernicus's new postulate inverted the traditional relationship of the Sun and the Earth, identifying the Sun as the center of the universe and the Earth as one of many solar satellites. Copernicus argued that spheres moved in endless; circular orbits. Since the universe and all the celestial bodies were thought to be spherical, he argued that their movements must also be circular and uniform (the Ptolemaic system considered the planets' circuits to be irregular). Copernicus reasoned that, since the movements of the planets appeared to be irregular, the Earth must not be the center of the universe. These discoveries were contrary to the views promulgated by the Roman Catholic Church. In fact, both Roman Catholics and Protestants suppressed any writings advocating these beliefs. When Galileo Galilei was brought to trial by the Roman Catholic Church for advocating the Copernican theory, he was forced to renounce his views.

GALILEO'S TELESCOPE

The telescope is thought to have been invented in 1609 by the Dutch optician Hans Lippershey but had no real scientific application until Galileo Galilei improved and adapted it to observe celestial bodies. Galileo's first telescope, made of a leather tube covered by a lens at each end (one lens convex and the other concave), magnified objects up to 30 times. Using the telescope, Galileo discovered that the Sun's surface had imperfections (sunspots), that the Moon had mountains and craters, and that there were four moons, or satellites, that traveled around Jupiter.

THE TRAVELERS

After many years and great advancements in technology, scientists decided that space observation conducted only from the Earth's surface was insufficient. In 1959, the first space probe was launched, an automatic vehicle that flew to the Moon and photographed its hidden face. The space probes Voyager 1 and 2 explored the planets Jupiter, Saturn, Uranus, and Neptune, a milestone in space exploration. In 2005, Voyager 1 reached the region called Termination Shock, the frontier of the solar system, representing the farthest region explored by humanity. Both probes carried with them golden discs, named Sounds of Earth, containing sounds and images portraying the diversity of life on Earth.

17th Century

Galileo Galilei
1564-1642

Built the first telescope, a primitive device with which he discovered sunspots, four of Jupiter's moons, the phases of Venus, and craters on the Moon's surface.

17th Century

Isaac Newton
1642-1727

He built upon the ideas of Galileo and developed the theory of universal gravitation, asserting that the movements of the Earth and the celestial bodies are governed by the same natural laws.

20th Century

Edwin Hubble
1889-1953

In 1929, he began to investigate the expansion of the galaxies, allowing scientists to obtain an idea of the true scale of the universe as well as refine the big bang theory.

Sprinkled with Stars

Constellations are groups of stars thought to represent different animals, mythological characters, and other figures. Constellations were invented by ancient civilizations to serve as reference points in the Earth's sky. There are 88 of these collections of stars. Although each star in a constellation appears related to the others, it is actually very far from them. Not all the constellations are visible at the same time from any one place on the Earth. ◉

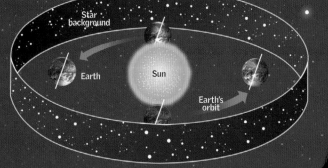

Chi1 Orionis
Xi Orionis
Mu Orionis
Betelgeu

ORIGIN

The history of western culture's constellations begins with the first astronomical observations made by ancient Mesopotamian peoples. Because we inherited the constellations from Greco-Roman culture, most of the constellations are named after figures in classical mythology. All of the earliest constellations were named by the 16th century. Constellations discovered more recently bear names drawn from science or technology or from exotic fauna discovered in various places across the globe.

23.5°

88
constellations

The Sky Changes

The Earth takes one year to orbit the Sun. As the planet advances in its orbit, the nighttime sky changes, allowing different parts of it to be seen. This is why some constellations can only be seen during certain seasons of the year. In addition, different constellations can be seen from different latitudes. Only near the equator is it possible to see all 88 constellations.

Star background

Earth

Sun

Earth's orbit

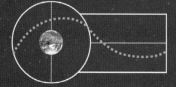

LEO
The brightest stars are those of the head and back. Regulus is prominent.

CANCER
is the least notable of the zodiac's constellations.

GEMINI
The stars Castor and Pollux form the head of the twins.

TAURUS
is visible even without binoculars. The brightest star, Aldebaran, is red.

ARIES
has only one very bright star, Hamal, the Arabic word for "sheep."

PISCES
Not a very noteworthy constellation, it has no very bright stars.

The Constellations of the Zodiac

The 13 constellations located within the elliptical plane—through which the Sun passes as seen from Earth—are called the constellations of the zodiac. Twelve of these constellations have long formed the foundation of astrology, but Ophiuchus, the 13th, is ignored by astrologers as a new addition.

OBSERVING THE CONSTELLATIONS

Observers in both hemispheres can see the constellations of the zodiac. In the Northern Hemisphere, the southern constellations, such as Scorpius, are difficult to see, and in the Southern Hemisphere, northern constellations, such as Gemini, are difficult to study.

Mythological Characters

Since ancient times, animal figures have been seen represented in the sky by groups of stars. The constellation of Taurus takes its name from its resemblance to a bull. Orion, Cassiopeia, Andromeda, and Perseus were named after characters of Greek tragedies.

Omicron Orionis

Heka

Pi2 Orionis

Bellatrix

Pi3 Orionis

Pi4 Orionis

THE MYSTERY OF GIZA
The alignment of the three pyramids at Giza in Egypt appears to be related to the alignment of the three stars of Orion's belt.

Pi5 Orionis

Pi6 Orionis

Mintaka

Alnilam

Alnitak

Saiph

Rigel

Different Cultures

In antiquity, each culture recognized certain constellations that other civilizations did not. The Chinese see smaller, more detailed patterns in the stars, allowing for more precise positional information. Various cultures also tend to use varied names for the same constellation. Scorpius is recognized by the people of Mesopotamia, Greece, Rome, Mesoamerica, and Oceania—under different names.

SCORPIUS
In Greco-Roman mythology, Orion and Scorpius are closely linked. Orion is the giant, handsome, seductive hunter.

URSA MAJOR
The bear represented by this constellation is unusual because of its long tail. The constellations' shapes rarely agree perfectly with their namesakes.

THE CENTAUR
is a creature from Greek mythology, half man and half horse. The centaur accompanied Orion during his quest to recover his sight.

13

OPHIUCHUS
Although it is the 13th constellation of the zodiac, Ophiuchus is not a part of the zodiac. When astrology began 3,000 years ago, the constellation was far from the zodiac.

Babylon

The Babylonians conceived of the zodiac 2,000 years ago as a way of measuring time, using it as a symbolic calendar.

LIBRA
was at one point, part of Scorpius.

SAGITTARIUS
is located at the center of the Milky Way and is full of nebulae and star groups.

AQUARIUS
as globular clusters nd nebulae visible with inoculars.

CAPRICORN
is one of the least prominent constellations.

SCORPIUS
lies in the direction of the Milky Way and its brightest star is Antares.

VIRGO
is a constellation with several bright stars.

Celestial Cartography

A s on the Earth, so in heaven. Just as terrestrial maps help us find locations on the surface of the planet, star charts use a similar coordinate system to indicate various celestial bodies and locations. Planispheres, or star wheels, are based on the idea of a celestial sphere (an imaginary globe on which the stars appear to lie and that surrounds the planet). Two common types are polar and bimonthly star maps.

THE CELESTIAL SPHERE

The celestial sphere is imagined to extend around the Earth and forms the basis for modern star cartography. The sphere is divided into a network of lines and coordinates corresponding to those used on the Earth, allowing an observer to locate constellations on the sphere. The celestial equator is a projection of the Earth's equator, the north and south celestial poles align with the axis of the Earth, and the elliptic coincides with the path along which the Sun appears to move.

Measuring Distances

Once a star or constellation has been located in the sky, hands and arms can serve as simple measuring tools. A single extended finger, shown in the first illustration, can form a one-degree angle from the observer's line of sight and is useful for measuring short distances between stars. The closed palm of the hand forms a 10° angle, and the open hand measures 20°.

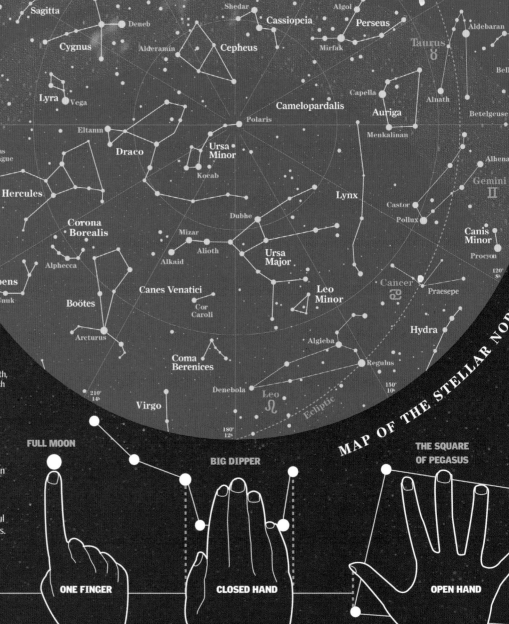

MAP OF THE STELLAR NO

FULL MOON

BIG DIPPER

THE SQUARE OF PEGASUS

ONE FINGER

CLOSED HAND

OPEN HAND

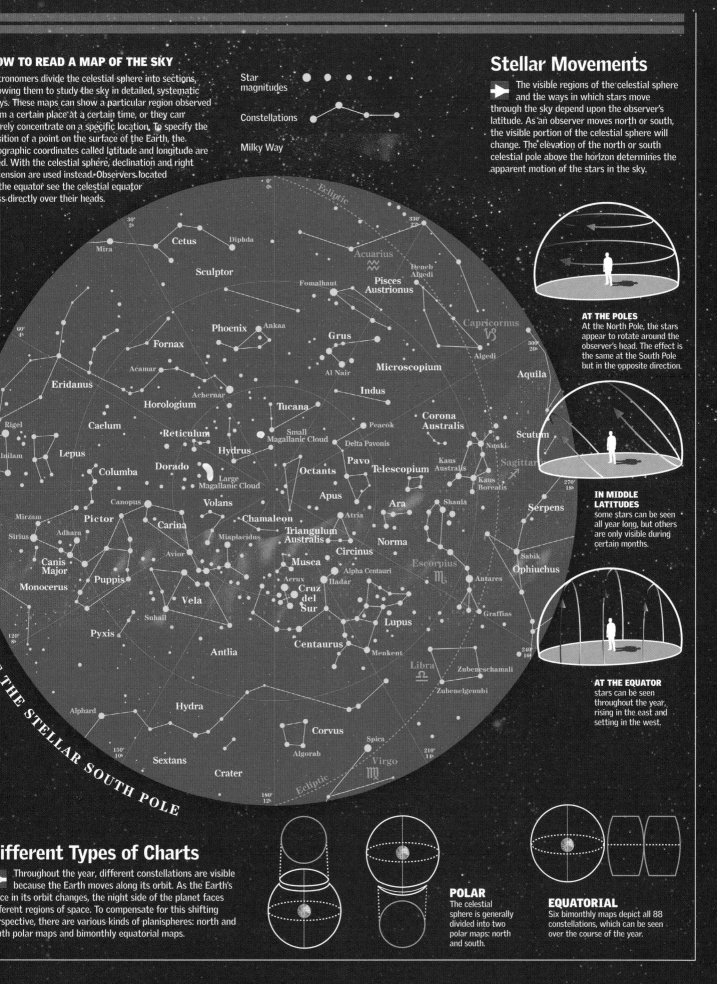

OW TO READ A MAP OF THE SKY

stronomers divide the celestial sphere into sections,
owing them to study the sky in detailed, systematic
ys. These maps can show a particular region observed
m a certain place at a certain time, or they can
rely concentrate on a specific location. To specify the
sition of a point on the surface of the Earth, the
ographic coordinates called latitude and longitude are
d. With the celestial sphere, declination and right
ension are used instead. Observers located
the equator see the celestial equator
s directly over their heads.

Star magnitudes

Constellations

Milky Way

Stellar Movements

The visible regions of the celestial sphere
and the ways in which stars move
through the sky depend upon the observer's
latitude. As an observer moves north or south,
the visible portion of the celestial sphere will
change. The elevation of the north or south
celestial pole above the horizon determines the
apparent motion of the stars in the sky.

AT THE POLES
At the North Pole, the stars
appear to rotate around the
observer's head. The effect is
the same at the South Pole
but in the opposite direction.

IN MIDDLE LATITUDES
some stars can be seen
all year long, but others
are only visible during
certain months.

AT THE EQUATOR
stars can be seen
throughout the year,
rising in the east and
setting in the west.

ifferent Types of Charts

Throughout the year, different constellations are visible
because the Earth moves along its orbit. As the Earth's
ce in its orbit changes, the night side of the planet faces
ferent regions of space. To compensate for this shifting
rspective, there are various kinds of planispheres: north and
th polar maps and bimonthly equatorial maps.

POLAR
The celestial
sphere is generally
divided into two
polar maps: north
and south.

EQUATORIAL
Six bimonthly maps depict all 88
constellations, which can be seen
over the course of the year.

From the Home Garden

S targazing is not difficult. After learning to locate celestial objects, many people find the hobby very gratifying. With the aid of a star map, you can recognize galaxies, nebulae, star clusters, planets, and other objects. Some of these treasures of the universe are visible with the unaided eye, but others require binoculars or even more sophisticated telescopes. Familiarity with the night sky is useful in many ways.

Basics

Before stepping out to observe the night sky, make sure you have everything you need. If you collect all your supplies beforehand, you will avoid having to expose your eyes to bright light once they have adjusted to darkness. In addition to binoculars, star maps, and a notebook, you should bring warm clothes, a comfortable seat, and something to drink.

Planisphere

Compass

Flashlight with red cellophane

How to Look at the Moon

Under various degrees of magnification, the Moon and stars take on different appearances. In some cases, you can make observations of the Moon with the unaided eye as well as with binoculars or a telescope.

Moon

Normal view

10 TIMES LARGER

View with binoculars

50 TO 100 TIMES LARGER

View with telescope

THE MOTION OF CONSTELLATIONS

The Earth's rotation makes the planets and stars appear to move through the nighttime sky in a general east-to-west direction. When the southern constellation Orion, visible from November through March, is viewed from the Northern Hemisphere, it appears to move from left to right.

12:00 A.M.

9:00 P.M.

JÚPITER

3:00 A.M.

ORIÓN

EAST

SOUTH

WEST

BARREL

OPTIC TUBE

TRIPOD ADAPTER

FOCUSING WHEEL

FOCUSING EYEPIECE

ADJUSTMENT SCREW

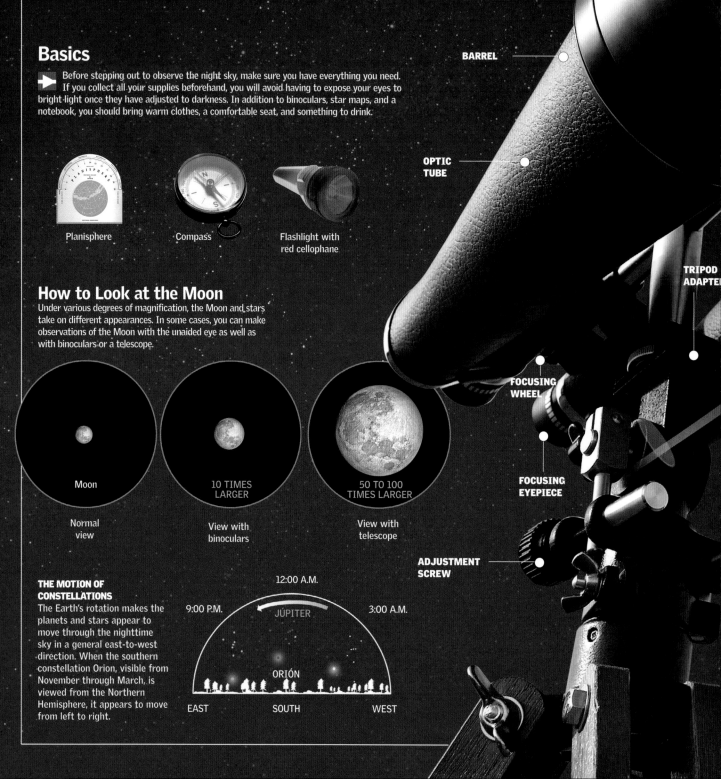

Observable Objects

The sky is a very busy place. Not only are there stars and planets, but there are also satellites, airplanes, comets, and meteorites. Fortunately all become recognizable by their appearance as well as their movement.

SHOOTING STARS
Very short flashes of light lasting only a fraction of a second

MOON
The illuminated face of the Moon can always be seen at some time during the night, at least partially, except around the new moon.

VENUS
can generally be seen above the horizon at dusk or dawn.

SATELLITES
The bigger ones are brighter than some stars. Some take a while to cross the sky.

COMETS
visible to the naked eye appear every one to two years and are visible for weeks or even months.

OBJECTIVE

PRISM

Flat Perspective

A constellation is a group of stars that, when viewed from a certain angle, seem to assume a specific shape. However, these stars that seem closely joined together are, in fact, separated by great distances.

17,000
LIGHT-YEARS FROM EARTH
OMEGA

4.2
LIGHT-YEARS FROM EARTH
CENTAURI

Measurement methods

A planisphere is a circular star chart that is used to locate celestial bodies in the celestial sphere. To identify a particular object, your own arms and body can be used to measure its direction and altitude in relation to the horizon.

MEASUREMENT OF ELEVATION

90°

Starting at the horizon, extend one of your arms until it is perpendicular to the other.

45°

Horizon

To measure a 45° angle, move your arm halfway up from the horizon.

MEASURING DIRECTION

90°

The planisphere indicates the principal direction of a star. Place the arms at 90º, using north or south as the base.

45°

A star to the southwest could be located with your arms at 45°. Combine the directional angles with your hand measurements for elevation.

A Four-Eyed Giant

The Paranal Observatory, one of the most advanced in the world, is located in the region of Antofagasta, Chile. It uses four identical telescopes to obtain enough light-gathering power that it could see the flame of a candle on the surface of the Moon. This sophisticated collection of digital cameras, reflecting mirrors, and other instruments is mounted in the interior of four metallic structures weighing hundreds of tons. The Very Large Telescope (VLT) is operated by a scientific consortium drawn from eight European countries. One of their stated objectives is to discover new worlds orbiting other stars.

CLIMATIC CONDITIONS

Cerro Paranal is located in the driest part of the Atacama desert, where the conditions for astronomical observation are extraordinarily favorable. It is an 8,645-foot- (2,635-m-) tall mountain that has about 350 cloudless nights a year.

10.9 (750)
LB PER SQ IN (MBAR)
Air pressure

0.06 (0.96)
LB PER CU FT (KG/M3)
Air density

18–77° (-8–25°)
FAHRENHEIT (CELSIUS)
Average temperature

5 to 20
PERCENT
Humidity

DOME
Its protective co
perceives change
in the weather b
means of therma
sensors.

ARMILLARY SPHERE
Invented by Eratosthenes in the year 225 BC, it was used as a teaching aid and became especially popular in the Middle Ages thanks to Danish astronomer Tycho Brahe.

2500–2000 BC
STONEHENGE
Located in Wiltshire, England, it is an observatory temple dating from the Neolithic Period.

435–455 BC
CARACOL
It is located in the ruins of the Mayan city of Chichén Itzá. The structure was used for venerating the Sun, the Moon, and Venus.

Telescope units

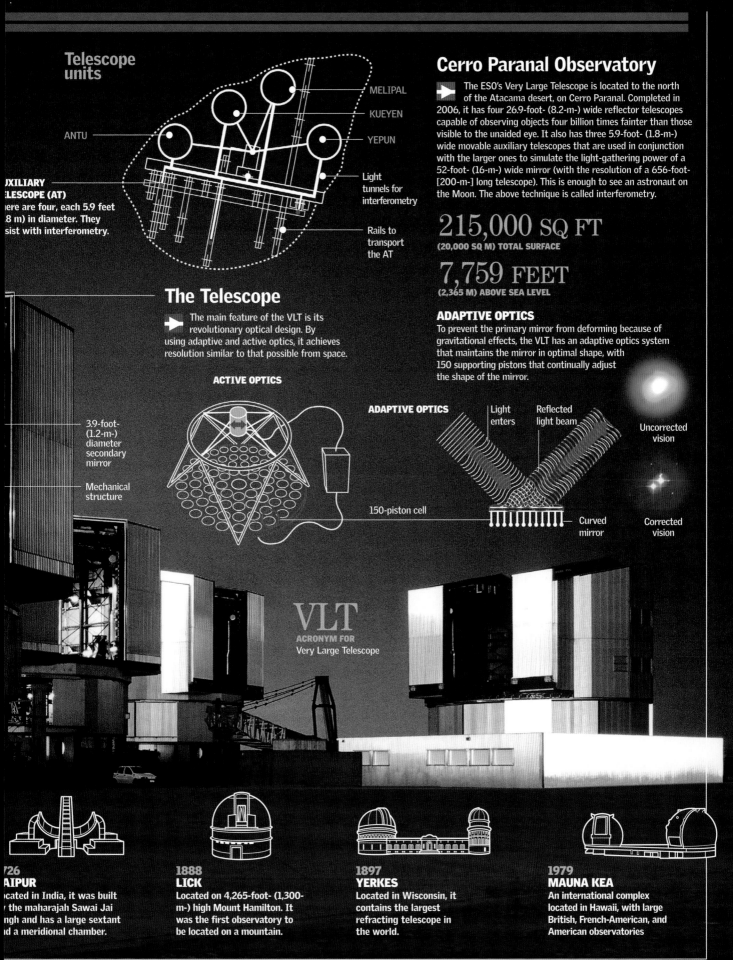

ANTU

MELIPAL

KUEYEN

YEPUN

Light tunnels for interferometry

Rails to transport the AT

AUXILIARY TELESCOPE (AT)
here are four, each 5.9 feet 8 m) in diameter. They sist with interferometry.

Cerro Paranal Observatory

The ESO's Very Large Telescope is located to the north of the Atacama desert, on Cerro Paranal. Completed in 2006, it has four 26.9-foot- (8.2-m-) wide reflector telescopes capable of observing objects four billion times fainter than those visible to the unaided eye. It also has three 5.9-foot- (1.8-m-) wide movable auxiliary telescopes that are used in conjunction with the larger ones to simulate the light-gathering power of a 52-foot- (16-m-) wide mirror (with the resolution of a 656-foot- [200-m-] long telescope). This is enough to see an astronaut on the Moon. The above technique is called interferometry.

215,000 SQ FT
(20,000 SQ M) TOTAL SURFACE

7,759 FEET
(2,365 M) ABOVE SEA LEVEL

ADAPTIVE OPTICS
To prevent the primary mirror from deforming because of gravitational effects, the VLT has an adaptive optics system that maintains the mirror in optimal shape, with 150 supporting pistons that continually adjust the shape of the mirror.

The Telescope

The main feature of the VLT is its revolutionary optical design. By using adaptive and active optics, it achieves resolution similar to that possible from space.

ACTIVE OPTICS

3.9-foot- (1.2-m-) diameter secondary mirror

Mechanical structure

ADAPTIVE OPTICS

Light enters

Reflected light beam

Uncorrected vision

150-piston cell

Curved mirror

Corrected vision

VLT
ACRONYM FOR
Very Large Telescope

726
AIPUR
cated in India, it was built the maharajah Sawai Jai ngh and has a large sextant d a meridional chamber.

1888
LICK
Located on 4,265-foot- (1,300-m-) high Mount Hamilton. It was the first observatory to be located on a mountain.

1897
YERKES
Located in Wisconsin, it contains the largest refracting telescope in the world.

1979
MAUNA KEA
An international complex located in Hawaii, with large British, French-American, and American observatories

Glossary

Annihilation

Total destruction of matter in a burst of energy, as when it encounters antimatter.

Antigravity

Hypothesized force, equal to gravity and diametrically opposed to it.

Antimatter

Matter formed from subatomic particles with shared properties. Its electrical charge is opposite that of normal matter.

Aperture

Diameter of the main mirror of a telescope or eyepiece. The larger the aperture, the more light the device receives.

Aphelion

The point in a celestial body's orbit farthest from the Sun. The Earth reaches aphelion on or about July 4, when it is 95,000,000 miles (152,600,000 km) from the Sun.

Apogee

The farthest position from the Earth reached by the Moon or any of the artificial satellites that orbit the planet.

Asteroids

Minor bodies of the solar system, formed by rock, metal, or a mixture of both. Most asteroids orbit the Sun between the orbits of Mars and Jupiter. Their size ranges from dozens of feet to hundreds of miles.

Astrolabe

Ancient astronomical instrument for measuring both the positions and the movements of celestial objects.

Astronomy

Science that studies the universe. It is concerned with the physical characteristics, movements, distances, formation, and interactions of galaxies, stars, planets, moons, comets, asteroids, and other celestial bodies.

Atmosphere

Layer of gas retained around a planet by its gravity. It is also the outer layer of matter in a star, where the energy produced in the star's interior is emitted in the form of radiation.

Atom

The smallest part of an element that partakes of all the element's properties. It is generally composed of three subatomic particles: the neutron, the proton, and the electron.

Aurora

Luminous phenomenon, with red and green layers, visible in the skies of the polar regions. The auroras are caused by the collision of solar particles with the Earth's atmosphere.

Austral

Related to the Southern Hemisphere.

Big Bang

Cosmological theory asserting that the universe began to exist as a result of a great explosion that occurred some 14 billion years ago.

Big Crunch

Cosmological theory asserting that the universe would undergo a final, complete collapse if it were to begin to contract.

Black Hole

Celestial body so dense that not even light can escape its gravity.

Black Hole, Stellar-Mass

Black hole produced by the explosion of a massive star as a supernova. Its mass is typically about 10 times that of the Sun.

Black Hole, Supermassive

Black hole located at the center of a galaxy and formed by material that falls into the central region of the galaxy. Its mass can be a billion times that of the Sun.

Carbon

One of the most common elements in the universe, produced by stars. All known life is carbon-based.

Chromosphere

The lowest layer of the Sun's atmosphere. It emits a pinkish-red light that can be seen only when the brighter photosphere is obscured during a total eclipse.

Circumpolar Star

Any star always visible to an observer on the Earth as it rotates about the celestial pole.

Comet

Object made of ice and rock dust. When a comet approaches the Sun, the growing heat causes the ice to evaporate, forming a gaseous head and a tail of dust and gas pointing away from the Sun.

Constellation

Group of stars in the sky. Constellations tend to bear the names of mythological characters or creatures. To astronomers, the constellations demarcate regions of the sky.

Core

In a planet, a solid, high-pressure central mass; in a star, the central region undergoing nuclear fusion; in a galaxy, the innermost light-years.

Corona

Upper atmosphere of the Sun. It is visible as a pearly halo during a total solar eclipse.

Cosmos

Another name for the universe.

Crater

Circular depression formed by the impact of

a meteorite on the surface of a natural satellite or a planet.

Crust

Rocky layer of the surface of a planet or natural satellite.

Curvature of Light

Distortion of light rays when passing through regions with strong gravitation.

Decay

Process by which radioactive elements and unstable particles become stable substances. Also the way in which black holes eventually disappear.

Density

Degree of solidity of a body (its mass divided by its volume).

Eclipse

Visual concealment of one celestial body by another. A lunar eclipse occurs when the Moon passes into the Earth's shadow, and a solar eclipse takes place when the Earth passes into the Moon's shadow.

Ecliptic

Imaginary line around the sky along which the Sun moves during the year. The orbits of the Earth and the other planets generally lie along the ecliptic.

Electrical Charge

Property of particles causing them to either attract or repel each other because of electrical forces. Electrical charges are either positive or negative.

Electromagnetic Radiation

Radiation composed of magnetic and electric fields moving at the speed of light. It encompasses radio waves (long wavelengths), visible light, and gamma rays (very short wavelengths).

Element

A basic substance of nature that cannot be diminished without losing its chemical properties. Each element (such as hydrogen, helium, carbon, oxygen) has its own characteristics.

Elliptical Orbit

Orbit shaped like a flattened circle. All orbits are elliptical. A circle is a special form of an ellipse.

Energy

The capacity to do work.

Event Horizon

The edge of a black hole.

Extraterrestrial

Foreign to the Earth.

Force

Something that changes the motion or shape of a body.

Galactic Filament

Structure formed by superclusters of galaxies stretching out through great portions of space. Filaments are the largest structures in the universe and are separated by great voids.

Galaxy

Collection of billions of stars, nebulae, dust, and interstellar gas held together by gravity.

Galaxy Cluster

Group of galaxies linked together by gravity.

Gamma Rays

Form of electromagnetic radiation with greatest energy and shortest wavelength. It is generated by only the most powerful phenomena in the universe, such as supernovae or the fusion of neutron stars.

General Relativity

Theory formulated by Albert Einstein in 1915. In part, it holds that gravity is a natural consequence of the curvature of space-time caused by the presence of a massive body. In general relativity, the phenomena of classical mechanics (such as the orbit of a planet or the fall of an object) are caused by gravity and are represented as inertial movements within space-time.

Gravitational Wave

Waves in space that travel at the speed of light and are produced by the movements of very massive bodies.

Gravity

Attractive force between bodies, such as between the Earth and the Moon.

Greenhouse Effect

Temperature increase caused by gases (such as carbon dioxide and methane) that prevent the surface heat of a planet from escaping into space.

Heliosphere

The region of space around the Sun in which its effects are evident. It extends some 100 astronomical units around the Sun.

Helium

The second most common and second lightest element in the universe. It is a product of the big bang and of nuclear fusion of stars.

Hubble Constant

Number that measures the rate of expansion of the universe. It is expressed in kilometers per second per millions of parsecs. It is currently estimated at 70 km/s/Mpc.

Hydrogen

The most common and lightest element in the universe; the main component of stars and galaxies.

Hypernova

Destruction of a massive star, which emits a wave of gamma rays extending great distances across the universe.

Implosion

Collapse of a body upon itself in response to great external pressure.

Infrared Radiation

Heat radiation, with a wavelength between visible light and radio waves.

Intergalactic Space

Space between galaxies.

Interstellar Space

Space between the stars.

Ionosphere

Region of the Earth's atmosphere that is electrically charged and is located between 30 and 370 miles (50 and 600 km) from the Earth's surface.

Kuiper Belt

Region of the solar system that is home to millions of frozen objects, such as comets. It stretches from the orbit of Neptune to the inner limit of the Oort cloud.

Light

Electromagnetic radiation with a wavelength visible to the human eye.

Light Pollution

Brightness of the sky originating in street illumination and other artificial lighting, which impedes the observation of dim celestial objects.

Light-Year

Standard astronomical measurement unit equivalent to the distance traveled by light, or any form of electromagnetic radiation, in one year. Equivalent to 6,000,000,000,000 miles (10,000,000,000,000 km).

Lunar Mare

The large, dark regions of the surface of the Moon. They were originally thought to be seas, but they are actually great depressions covered by lava.

Magnetic Field

The area near a magnetic body, electric current, or changing electric field. Planets, stars, and galaxies have magnetic fields that extend into space.

Magnetosphere

Sphere that surrounds a planet with a magnetic field strong enough to protect the planet from the solar wind.

Mantle

Layer that lies between the crust and the core of a planet.

Mass

Measure of the amount of matter in an object.

Matter

The substance of a physical object, it occupies a portion of space.

Meteorite

Rocky or metallic object that strikes the surface of a planet or satellite, where it can form a crater.

Milky Way

The galaxy to which the Sun and the solar system belong. It is visible as a pale band of light that crosses our night sky.

Molecule

Smallest unit of a pure substance that has the composition and chemical properties of the substance. It is formed by one or more atoms.

Moon

The Earth's natural satellite is called the Moon. The natural satellites of other planets are commonly known as moons and have their own proper names.

Nebulae

Clouds of gas and dust in space. Nebulae can be seen when they reflect starlight or when they obstruct light from sources behind them.

Neutron

Electrically neutral subatomic particle. It makes up part of an atom's nucleus (with the exception of ordinary hydrogen).

Neutron Star

Collapsed star consisting mostly of neutrons.

Nova

Star that increases greatly in brightness for several days or weeks and then slowly fades. Most novae probably occur in binary-star systems in which a white dwarf draws in matter from its companion star.

Nuclear Fusion

Nuclear reaction in which relatively light elements (such as hydrogen) form heavier elements (such as helium). Nuclear fusion is the source of energy that makes stars shine.

Oxygen

Chemical element vital to life and to the expansion of the universe. Oxygen makes up 21 percent of the Earth's atmosphere.

Particle

In particle physics, a tiny, individual component of matter with characteristic mass, electrical charge, and other properties.

Perihelion

The point in a celestial body's orbit closest to the Sun. The Earth reaches perihelion on or about

January 4, when it is 92,000,000 miles (147,500,000 km) from the Sun.

Photon

Elemental particle responsible for electromagnetic radiation. Photons are the most common particles in the universe.

Planet

Roughly spherical object made of rocks or gas orbiting a star. A planet cannot generate its own light but reflects the light of its parent star.

Polestar

Polaris, a star that lies near the celestial north pole. Polaris is commonly called the North Star. Over thousands of years, other stars will become the polestar.

Proton

Subatomic particle with positive electrical charge. It forms part of the nucleus of an atom.

Radio Galaxy

Active galaxy emitting energy as both radio waves and light. Most of the radio emission originates at the core of the galaxy.

Solar Flare

Immense explosion produced on the surface of the Sun by the collision of two loops of the solar magnetic field.

Solar Mass

Standard unit of mass against which other objects in the universe can be compared. The Sun has 333,000 times as much mass as the Earth.

Space

The medium through which all celestial bodies move.

Space-Time

Four-dimensional conception of the universe in which length, width, and height constitute three dimensions and time acts as the fourth.

Spectral Analysis

Study of spectral lines that provide information about the composition of stars or galaxies and their redshifts.

Spectrum

The result of dispersing the electromagnetic radiation of an object so that the wavelengths of which it is composed can be seen. Dark lines that originate from elements that are present and punctuate the spectrum at specific wavelengths reveal the composition of the object.

Speed of Light

The distance traveled by light in a vacuum in one second (approximately 186,000 miles, or 300,000 km). No object can move faster than the speed of light.

Star

Enormous sphere of gas (generally hydrogen) that radiates light and heat. The Sun is a star.

Star Cluster

Group of stars linked together by gravity. Open clusters are scattered groups of several hundred stars. Globular clusters are dense spheres of several million old stars.

Sunspots

Dark, relatively cool spots on the surface of the Sun. They tend to be located on either side of the solar equator and are created by the solar magnetic field.

Supernova

Explosion of a massive star at the end of its life.

Tide

The effect of the gravitational pull of one astronomical object upon the surface of another. Ocean tides on Earth are an example.

Unstable

Tendency to change from one state into another less energetic one. Radioactive elements decay into more stable elements.

Vacuum

Space occupied by little or no matter.

Van Allen Belt

Radiation zone surrounding the Earth, where the Earth's magnetic field traps solar particles.

Wavelength

Distance between the peaks of any wave of electromagnetic radiation. Radiation with a short wavelength (such as X-rays) has more energy than radiation with a longer wavelength (such as radio waves).

Zenith

Point in the sky 90° above the horizon (that is, immediately above an observer).

Zodiac

Twelve constellations through which the Sun, the Moon, and the planets appear to move.

Index